→INTRODUCING

AMERICAN POLITICS

LAURA LOCKER & JULES SCHEELE

This edition published in the UK and the USA
in 2020 by Icon Books Ltd,
Omnibus Business Centre,
39–41 North Road,
London N7 9DP
email: info@iconbooks.com
www.iconbooks.com

Sold in the UK, Europe and Asia
by Faber & Faber Ltd,
Bloomsbury House,
74–77 Great Russell Street,
London WC1B 3DA
or their agents

Distributed in the UK, Europe and Asia
by Grantham Book Services,
Trent Road, Grantham NG31 7XQ

Distributed in South Africa
by Jonathan Ball,
Office B4, The District,
41 Sir Lowry Road,
Woodstock 7925

Distributed in Australia and New Zealand
by Allen & Unwin Pty Ltd,
PO Box 8500,
83 Alexander Street,
Crows Nest, NSW 2065

Distributed in the USA
by Publishers Group West,
1700 Fourth Street,
Berkeley, CA 94710

Distributed in Canada
by Publishers Group Canada,
76 Stafford Street, Unit 300
Toronto, Ontario M6J 2S1

Distributed in India
by Penguin Books India,
7th Floor, Infinity Tower – C,
DLF Cyber City, Gurgaon 122002,
Haryana

Previously published in 2018 as
American Politics: A Graphic History

ISBN: 978-178578-602-0

Originating editor: Kiera Jamison

Printed and bound in Great Britain
by Clays Ltd, Elcograf S.p.A.

PART I: THE FOUNDATIONS

In this book we will consider governmental institutions as the product of a mutually transformative interaction between state and society. Politics doesn't happen in a vacuum. As we will see, the ways in which the American government decides on laws and policies depends upon the mindset of the citizens, which is in turn shaped by their political socialization, their relationship to media, the influence of lobbyist and interest groups that have the money to sway ideas, and so forth. In this book, you will meet a diverse group of voters (and non-voters) who, through their engagement with the ideas central to American politics at a personal level, exemplify the American motto, "*e pluribus unum*" or "out of many, one."

AMERICAN POLITICAL CULTURE

We often talk about "American values," but what are these shared values that set the US apart from other nations? And can we say that there is a definable set of "core values" that most Americans share, given the vast diversity of beliefs and understandings in the nation? While there are many political subcultures in the US, there are indeed certain ideas, institutionalized in the Constitution, that shape how Americans view their economic, political, and personal lives, regardless of their political affiliation. What are some values that are generally shared in the United States?

THE EVOLUTION OF CORE VALUES

These core values have been interpreted differently though history. While the **Declaration of Independence** (1776) declared that "all men are created equal," equality in the United States meant something very different at the time of the ratification of the Constitution (1787) than it does today. For example, slavery was not abolished until 1865, 246 years after slaves were first brought to America, and it wasn't until the passage of the **Voting Rights Act** (1965) that most African Americans truly gained not just the right but the ability to vote. Before that, "Jim Crow" laws (at the time, "Jim Crow" was a derisive slang term for a black man) in the South were based on white supremacist ideologies, and they enforced segregation between whites and blacks.

POLITICAL IDEOLOGY

While we can identify shared, "core" values that are more or less widely held, there are many values that are interpreted differently by, or are unique to, different groups in society. These values tend to be bundled into a political ideology, which provides a roadmap with which we make sense of our world. A political ideology can be held by an individual or a group, but it tends to contain values, understandings, and beliefs about how the political and social world can and should work. In the United States, as in many parts of the world, we can broadly divide political ideologies into two different camps: **liberal** (also referred to as "**left-wing**") and **conservative** (or "**right-wing**"). Both ideologies have economic and social components. Unlike other nations, we do not have widely-shared communist or socialist ideologies.

SOCIAL LIBERALISM

We can divide liberalism in terms of its social and economic components, although the two often go hand-in-hand. Social liberals believe in **equality of opportunity** – everyone has the same access to economic, social, and political opportunities – and, to some degree, **equality of results** – opportunity leads to more equal social and material conditions. They feel that government can play a key role in promoting both.

Social policy tends to inform economic policy, as, for example, through government programs to aid poor and marginalized members of society. Social liberals tend to be in favor of **affirmative action**: government policies that give advantage to groups which have historically faced discrimination. Other key liberal social issues include upholding access to abortion, protecting immigrant rights, restricting gun access, protecting same-sex marriage, abolishing the death penalty, providing universal health care, and protecting the environment.

ECONOMIC LIBERALISM

Modern economic liberalism in the United States is quite different from the "liberalism" of classic economic theory or of other modern nations. Liberal economic theory, based on the ideas of the economist **Adam Smith** (1723–90), believes in the power of a market entirely free from regulation, with open economic borders, and in the idea that people are naturally inclined to "truck, barter, and exchange." Modern American liberals deviate from this, believing that the government's role is to intervene in the market to correct for the human and economic toll of "unbridled capitalism."

This ideology came to full fruition in the wake of the Great Depression (1929–39). During this time, the economist **John Maynard Keynes** (1883–1946) inspired what was known as the Keynesian Revolution, and governments around the world (including that of Franklin D. Roosevelt) began to adopt his policy recommendation that **deficit spending** – where government spending exceeds revenue – was not only okay but necessary for economic recovery and growth.

FDR CREATED JOBS FOR MILLIONS BY SETTING UP PUBLIC WORKS PROGRAMS, BUILDING SCHOOLS, PARKS, HOSPITALS AND ROADS.

BLUE RIDGE PARKWAY
FRANKLIN D. ROOSEVELT
HOOVER DAM

SOCIAL CONSERVATISM

Generally, conservatism centers around a preference for tradition and social order, and a distrust of change. It can look very different from one country to the next, as what is perceived as "traditional" differs culturally and historically. Universally, social conservatism tends to be rooted in religious moralism. The majority of social conservatives in the US are Christians and tend to vote Republican. They are firmly against abortion and would like to overturn *Roe v. Wade* (1973), the landmark ruling that affirmed a woman's right to have access to abortions. They also share an opposition to same-sex marriage and support the 1996 **Defense of Marriage Act** (DOMA), signed into law by President Bill Clinton, which defined marriage as being only between one man and one woman. (The act was declared unconstitutional by the Supreme Court ruling *United States v. Windsor* in 2013.)

ECONOMIC CONSERVATISM

Traditional economic conservatives keep their eye on the government's budget, seeing many government programs as wasteful. They echo the classic economic liberal view that the economy works best when it is less regulated, and they find the ideas behind Keynesian economics, with its belief that politicians can stimulate growth through government spending, fairly repugnant. They generally focus on fewer government regulations, lower taxes, and economic and fiscal policies aimed at promoting the growth of business and reducing the barriers to trade. Strains of economic conservatism can be found in all of the major parties. It was actually during the presidency of Democrat Bill Clinton (1993–2001) that the nation experienced its largest budget surplus in history.

OVERLAPPING MEMBERSHIPS

Many people sit more on an ideological spectrum than rigidly defining themselves as "liberal" or "conservative." These people have "overlapping memberships." Take, for example, a woman (who tend to be more liberal), who is deeply religious (tending towards conservatism), the parent of a disabled child (relying on "liberal" social programs and safety nets), and from a military family (tending towards conservatism). Her "membership" in each of these groups makes her overall ideology more complicated and difficult to categorize. Different parts of her identity may be "activated" by different ideological messages.

A DIVIDED NATION?

The presidential election of 2016 left many with the feeling that the nation was deeply divided. Among liberals, debates ran hot between supporters of Bernie Sanders and Hillary Clinton. Some conservative voters were uneasy with Donald Trump's rhetoric towards women, the disabled, and immigrants, among other groups, and some doubted his sincerity towards conservative, traditional values. Trump's election was met with large protests throughout the nation, which were exacerbated by his issuance of controversial executive orders soon after his taking office. Both sides sought to send the message that their party was the true defender of American core values. The Democratic Party stated, "This election is about more than Democrats and Republicans. It is about who we are as a nation, and who we will be in the future."

POLITICAL PARTIES

While the level of **partisanship** (a strong bias or prejudice towards a particular party) in the United States can seem overwhelming at times, political parties do play an important role in the American political process. They act as an intermediary between politicians and the people, bundling information and ideological stances into a **political platform** – a formal declaration of principles – with which individuals can affiliate themselves. Parties can simplify choice and make the voting process easier. We may know nothing about a candidate for office but, based on their party affiliation, we can usually make a number of assumptions about their stance on key issues.

EVOLUTION OF POLITICAL PARTIES

While it's hard to imagine a time when parties didn't play such a strong role in American politics, when the Constitution was written there were no formal political parties, although people identified as **Federalists** (in favor of a stronger centralized government) or **Anti-Federalists** (strong proponents of state rights). The earliest parties were the Federalists and the **Democratic Republicans**. Since then, they've experienced a few evolutions. The Federalist party died out after an unpopular opposition to the War of 1812.

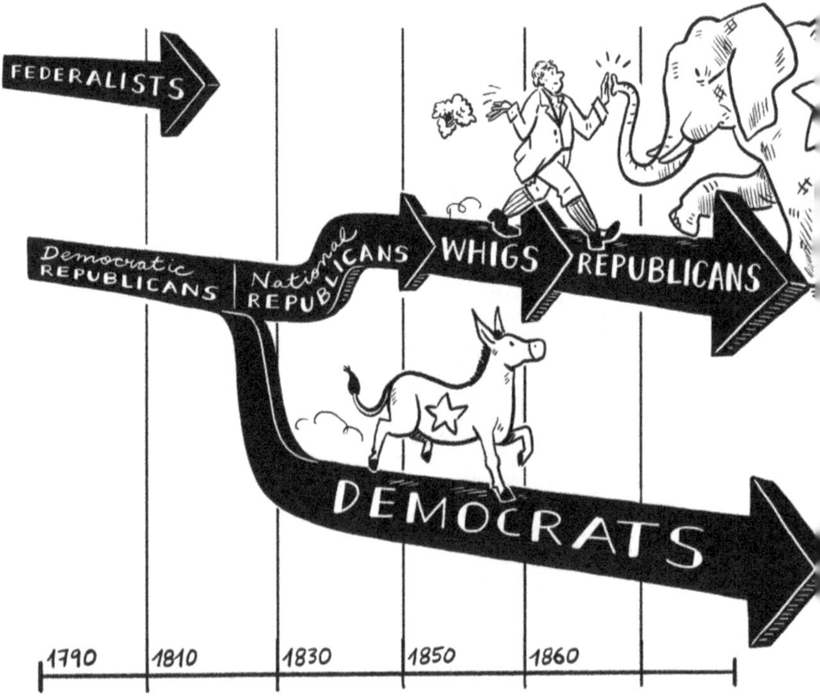

By 1828, the Democratic Republicans split in two: the Democratic Republicans (led by **Andrew Jackson**, who would become president the following year) and the **National Republicans** (led by John Quincy Adams, the president at the time). In 1834, the National Republican Party dissolved and the **Whig party** became prominent. The Whigs elected two presidents before merging with a third party called the **Free-Soilers** to form the **Republican Party**, electing **Abraham Lincoln** as president in 1861. While the Civil War (1861–5) brought about some factioning, the Democrats and Republicans remain the two dominant parties today.

POLITICAL PARTIES AND MACHINE POLITICS

We can't talk about the evolution of parties without understanding that for over 150 years they controlled the democratic process in a way that seems rather, well, undemocratic. From the late 18th century, party-based political "machines" ran many major cities. Typically, the **political machine** exchanged favors for the voter's acquiescence in matters of public policy. It had a tight hierarchy, led by the "boss," with agents throughout the grassroots level. Immigrants, particularly the Irish, comprised a large part of the machine's base. George W. Plunkitt, leader of New York City's Tammany Hall Democratic machine, defended the system, arguing that through graft – using politics for personal gain by leveraging the jobs, contracts, and "gifts" available through government spending – he was able to further the interests of the party, the city, voters, and, of course, himself. As immigration declined and the middle class grew, opposition to the machine gained force. By the 1940's, most machines were in a state of collapse.

THE REPUBLICAN PARTY

The Republican Party, known as the "**GOP**" (**Grand Old Party**), was originally an anti-slavery party. After the election of Abraham Lincoln, it was dominant, winning 8 of the next 12 races for president, but if we conjure an image of the iconic conservative Republican president, we may well think of Ronald Reagan (President: 1981–9).

"UNTIL SOMEONE CAN PROVE THE UNBORN HUMAN IS NOT ALIVE, WE MUST GIVE IT THE BENEFIT OF THE DOUBT AND ASSUME IT IS. AND THUS, IT SHOULD BE ENTITLED TO LIFE, LIBERTY, AND THE PURSUIT OF HAPPINESS."
"I AM PRO-LIFE, AND I WILL BE APPOINTING PRO-LIFE JUDGES."
"I BELIEVE IN THE IDEA OF AMNESTY FOR THOSE WHO HAVE PUT DOWN ROOTS AND WHO HAVE LIVED HERE, EVEN THOUGH SOMETIME BACK THEY MAY HAVE ENTERED ILLEGALLY."
"IT'S OUR RIGHT, AS A SOVEREIGN NATION, TO CHOOSE IMMIGRANTS THAT WE THINK ARE THE LIKELIEST TO THRIVE AND FLOURISH AND LOVE US."
Today's Republican Party has a complex voter base, who see it as the protector of conservative values, smaller government, and patriotic sentiment. Among other things, Rep. President Donald Trump campaigned to end Obama's Affordable Care Act, to greatly expand the military, and to build a wall between the US and Mexico to reduce illegal immigration – all as part of his promise to "make America great again."

What is the demographic breakdown of the modern Republican Party? In 2016, 57% of white voters supported Trump, compared to 8% of black voters, 28% of Latino voters, and 27% of Asian voters. Support had increased in the previous ten years among white men, particularly those without a college degree. 25% of Republican voters are 65 or older. However, statistics show that by 2044 whites will be in the minority in the US, so the Republican Party may have to find a way to appeal to minority voters in order to remain dominant.

THE REPUBLICAN PARTY PLATFORM

The Republican Party platform, like the party itself, has evolved over time. Its first party platform, written in 1856, focused on slavery, declaring it antithetical to the "inalienable right to life, liberty, and the pursuit of happiness" of all members of the nation. The contemporary party platform opens with an appeal to nationalism, stating, "We believe in **American exceptionalism**. We believe the United States of America is unlike any other nation on earth." Among other things, the party is grounded in beliefs in lower taxes, conservative values, greater rights for states, gun rights, tighter borders, military strength, and an "America first" policy in international relations.

REPUBLICAN AFRICAN-AMERICAN VOTERS

Today, fewer than 10% of African American voters identify as Republican. In the past it was seen as the party of Lincoln, the Emancipator (of the slaves), and so was the preferred party of African Americans, particularly in the South.

The mechanization of farming in the 1920's–40's reduced the need for laborers, which meant many African Americans moved north to seek economic opportunity. Many also moved in search of personal and political freedoms, a movement known as the Great Black Migration. Party alignments began to shuffle. The Democratic Party became the party of the New Deal (a movement we'll talk about shortly) and increasingly courted minority voters. In contrast, the Republican Party courted white voters in the South, who generally opposed policies to advance the interests of black voters. From 1968 onwards, the majority of the 16 states of the Southern voting bloc would vote Republican in presidential elections, and the party held solid control of state and local offices as well.

THE REPUBLICAN PARTY AND THE NATIONAL RIFLE ASSOCIATION

As a staunch defender of a broad interpretation of the 2nd Amendment right of Americans to keep and bear arms, the relationship between the Republican Party and the National Rifle Association is close. The NRA backed Donald Trump in 2016, spending more on his endorsement than any other outside group – three times as much as it spent backing Mitt Romney in 2012. The GOP party platform states: "We uphold the right of individuals to keep and bear arms, a natural inalienable right that predates the Constitution and is secured by the 2nd Amendment. Lawful gun ownership enables Americans to exercise their God-given right of self-defense for the safety of their homes, their loved ones, and their communities." Donald Trump personally addressed the NRA after becoming president and was the first sitting president to do so since Ronald Reagan.

THE DEMOCRATIC PARTY

The Democratic Party is the world's oldest existing political party, originally referring to itself as "Republicans" or "Jeffersonian Republicans." Democrats stand for a strict separation of church and state, gay rights, gun control, strengthening social safety nets, access to abortion, environmental regulation, a relaxed view towards immigration, and generally a preference for "progressive" social change. With the election of Barack Obama in 2008, there was a feeling of optimism that the Democratic Party could capture a broad spectrum of the voting electorate. However, in 2016, although Hillary Clinton won the popular vote by over 2.8 million votes, she lost the electoral college vote, and Republicans gained the majority in both the House and Senate.

Of all registered voters, 48% identify as Democratic. The ethnic and racial breakdown of those who identify as Democrats (or lean Democratic) is:

- 39% of whites
- 87% of African Americans
- 66% of Asians
- 63% of Hispanics.

54% of women identify or lean Democratic. Democrats tend to be more highly educated, capturing 55% of the voting public with a greater than high school education.

The Democratic Party hasn't always been a progressive party and in its early history held views that we more typically associate with the current Republican Party. It was with the election of Franklin D. Roosevelt in 1932 that the party became closer to what it is today. Democratic presidencies strengthened social safety nets (Social Security and the G.I. Bill), promoted civil rights (Civil Rights Act and the Voting Rights Act), and broadened access to healthcare (Affordable Care Act).

The Democrats have historically had a strong showing in Congress (we'll get into the functions of Congress later on in this book), particularly the House of Representatives, where it was the majority party for all but 4 years in a 62-year period (1930–94).

EQUAL
Opportunity
AND
HUMAN
DIGNITY

SURE, THE CIVIL RIGHTS ACT WAS SIGNED INTO LEGISLATION BY A DEMOCRATIC PRESIDENT, BUT THE STORY ISN'T THAT SIMPLE.
18 SOUTHERN DEMOCRATIC SENATORS, JOINED BY JUST ONE REPUBLICAN, LED A FILIBUSTER TO TRY TO PREVENT ITS PASSAGE.

THE DEMOCRATIC PARTY PLATFORM

The first Democratic Party platform, written in 1840, was a terse document that focused almost exclusively on limiting the powers of the federal government. The contemporary Democratic Party platform clearly shows the evolution of the party towards a belief that the government's duty is to actively intervene to promote its view of what constitutes American core values. It squarely aligns the party with economic justice for politically, economically, and socially marginalized members of the nation, diversity as strength, increased taxation of the wealthy, and an affirmation of the dangers of climate change. Like the Republican platform, it seeks to set the party apart from its rival parties in a clear and forceful manner.

THIRD PARTIES: A WASTED VOTE OR A NECESSITY?

We tend to think of the US as bipartisan, but independent third parties play a role in the political machine,, albeit a smaller one than in many other democratic countries, like Germany or India, where coalitions between multiple parties are the norm. In fact, 35% of voters in the US identify as independent. However, when a third-party candidate runs for a major political office, they often face criticism for being an election "spoiler," and their supporters for "wasting a vote." This was the case in 2000, when **Green Party** candidate Ralph Nader won 2.74% of the popular vote in the nail-bitingly close contest between Al Gore and George W. Bush, and again in the 2016 election, which saw a significant increase in votes for third-party candidates.

THIRD PARTIES: BARRIERS TO ELECTION

In the US, there is no constitutional limit to the number of parties that can vie for power, but barriers exist to their gaining power. Our system of "winner takes all" elections, where presidential candidates with the greatest number of votes in a state win all of the electoral votes, makes it harder for smaller parties to win any. This system contrasts with **proportional representation**, where seats in a political body are allocated according to the proportion of the vote garnered. To participate in presidential debates, candidates must show that they have at least 15% of voters supporting them. In some states, candidates have to gain a certain number of signatures of support before they are allowed on the ballot.

THE LIBERTARIAN PARTY

The Libertarian Party, founded in 1971, is the largest independent party in the US. It comes closer than any other party in standing for the purest expression of Adam Smith's **free market society**, which sees the government's only role in the economy as protecting property rights, adjudicating disputes, and protecting free trade. Libertarian thought is centered on the right of the individual to live as they want, as long as they don't tread on the right of others to live as they want. Currently, 122 Libertarians hold office in the US, primarily at the local level.

GREEN PARTY

Green parties became a political force in the United States in the 1990's, standing for environmentalism, nonviolence, social justice, participatory grassroots democracy, gender equality, LGBT rights, anti-war, and anti-racism. Ralph Nader, a political activist who rose to prominence after raising awareness about corporate negligence in the auto industry, was the movement's first presidential candidate, winning just 0.71% of the vote in 1996 but increasing to 2.74% in 2000. Jill Stein, a medical doctor turned activist, ran in 2012, earning 0.36% of the total vote, and in 2016, 1.07%. While they are the fourth largest party in the US, they hold fewer than 200 lower-level elected offices.

THE PEW CENTER TYPOLOGY

Another way of thinking of the partisan composition of the US is in terms of **partisan adherence** (how strongly an individual is loyal to one party or another) and political engagement. The Pew Center for Social Research engages in comprehensive surveys of political values, and its latest typology shows that a large number of individuals either do not strictly adhere to one party affiliation, or are not participating or interested in the political process.

Voting and aligning oneself with parties isn't the only way people engage with politics. As we go about our daily lives, our actions are constantly being shaped by political rules and **institutions**. Institutions are the "rules of the game" for society, which shape human interaction, and they can be both formal and informal. While no society can exist without institutions, it's important to note that they are not always efficient or fair and can be costly to change, leading to **institutional stickiness** – the persistence of an institution even if it no longer provides for optimal outcomes.

POLITICAL SOCIALIZATION

Informal institutions – codes of conduct, norms of behavior, and conventions – can be much harder to describe than formal ones. It's much easier to describe a constitution than the complex social dynamics of a gang in Chicago. Yet they are as important as formal institutions. We know informal institutions hold great influence, in part because if you took the same formal institutional structure – same constitution, same rule of law, etc. – and imposed it on a different society, you would have very different outcomes.

One of the key ways that informal institutions persist over time is through **political socialization**, a process that happens throughout our lifetime as social forces, such as our families, neighborhoods, schools, religion, the media, and others, work to shape our political outlook and values.

THE CONSTITUTION

It isn't always that case that you start with informal rules and that formal rules develop out of them. The process can move both ways. Formal rules can also complement and increase the effectiveness of informal institutions. The American Constitution, which is among the oldest living constitutions is the world, is an excellent example of formal rules that set the stage for the evolution of informal rules, ideas, and conventions in society.

The Constitution is considered the supreme law of the land, and it outlines the rights and responsibilities of the government and residents of the United States. It's relatively brief, comprising only 17 articles and a Bill of Rights.

ESTABLISHING FEDERALISM

Of course, the Constitution itself was shaped by shared norms and understandings that existed at the time it was written. One particularly strong influence was the belief that government authority should be limited. The Constitution started with the Articles of Confederation, which established the United States as a **confederation**, a governmental organization that unites states or territories for a common purpose but allows them to retain their sovereign authority. The states quickly realized that the negligible authority given to the central government under the Articles was not sufficient to resolve international or domestic issues that were challenging the new nation. However, they were wary of a **unitary** form of state, with power concentrated in the central government. In contrast, the Constitution established a **federal** form of government, where power was shared between the central government and the states.

EXPRESS AND IMPLIED POWERS

While a federal system implies a sharing of power between the central government and the states, how much power to give to each has been a key question since the founding of the union. The powers granted to the federal government by the Constitution are of two types: express and implied. **Express powers** are explicitly stated by the Constitution, while **implied powers** can be assumed to be included within their express counterparts. For example, the Constitution does not give the government the right to form a national bank, but it does give it permission to "coin money [and] regulate the value thereof," and so it is reasonable to assume that, in order to fulfill this commandment, the federal government may form a national bank.

POWERS OF THE STATE GOVERNMENT: RESERVED POWERS

The 10th Amendment to the Constitution was included to ensure that any powers not expressly delegated to the central government would be reserved for the states. Sometimes that causes a conflict between state and federal law, as has been the case with the legalization of marijuana in some states, while possession of the drug remains a crime at the federal level.

AMENDING THE CONSTITUTION: PROCEDURES

Technically, there are two ways by which the Constitution can be amended, although only one has ever been used. In that procedure, two-thirds of the House and Senate must approve of the proposal and send it to the state legislatures for a vote: a process known as **ratification**. Then, three-fourths of the state legislatures (today, 38 states) must affirm the proposed amendment. While at least 11,000 amendments have been proposed by Congress over the years, only 27 have ever been passed, 10 of those comprising the Bill of Rights. The last time the Constitution was amended was in 1992 with the passage of the 27th Amendment, which stated that any changes in the salaries of members of Congress could only take effect after the next term of office. This was actually one of the 12 original amendments by James Madison that had been rejected for ratification, 202 years earlier.

Dueling Ban Amendment
Prohibiting any person involved in a duel from holding federal office
We The People Amendment
Abolish doctrines of corporate personhood
Every Vote Counts Amendment
Abolish the electoral college

THE SUPREME COURT AND CONSTITUTIONAL INTERPRETATION

If the Constitution only changed through the formal amendment process, change would be slow in coming. Through the Supreme Court, rapid and sometimes dramatic change can be effected. The Court cannot amend the Constitution but, through its judgments as the final arbitrator of the law, it can make broad changes in how the law is interpreted, in a process known as **judicial review**. The Court's rulings can invalidate state or federal laws or **executive actions** (laws or rules put into place through unilateral presidential action) that are seen as in violation of constitutional laws and protections. This power was established in the landmark case of *Marbury v. Madison* (1803), which marked the first time that the Supreme Court declared an Act of Congress unconstitutional, thereafter establishing the judiciary as a power equal to the executive and legislative branches. We will discuss the Supreme Court in more detail in the next part of this book.

THE BILL OF RIGHTS

The 17 articles of the Constitution set the "rules of the game" for how government works. The Bill of Rights has come, over time, to do the same for the interaction not only between government and its people but also between the people themselves. It guarantees free speech, for example; although not all speech is protected, particularly when it puts others in danger. One still cannot yell "fire" in a crowded room and instigate a panic where people could be hurt.

Americans tend to think that the Bill of Rights is more encompassing than it is: according to a 2015 Annenberg Public Policy Center poll, 34% believe it gives one the right to own their own home. While this right doesn't appear in the Bill of Rights, the 10 amendments do encompass a broad range of freedoms and guarantees, the meaning and enforcement of which have been solidified over the years through landmark Supreme Court cases.

WE ALL EXERCISE OUR RIGHTS IN DIFFERENT WAYS.

WE MAY NOT LIKE EVERYTHING OTHER PEOPLE DO.

BUT WE RESPECT THEIR CONSTITUTIONAL RIGHT TO DO SO.
DEFEND DACA

THE BILL OF RIGHTS: HISTORY

The inclusion of a Bill of Rights in the Constitution was first an afterthought and, then, controversial. The Constitutional Convention (1787) – the meeting at which the Constitution was drafted – was drawing to a close when **George Mason**, a retired politician from Virginia suggested adding a bill of rights. His proposal was rejected. It was only under pressure from the Anti-Federalists that **James Madison**, a Federalist, eventually drafted a set of 19 amendments, of which 10 were eventually ratified by the states three years later.

DUE PROCESS

Half of the Bill of Rights is dedicated to protecting the rights of individuals who have been accused of a crime. Why is this necessary? For one, ensuring **due process** – that people accused of a crime have the right to be treated fairly – is a key component of ensuring that a government can't use the legal system to punish dissenters. **Procedural due process** refers not to the substance of the laws but rather to how laws are applied. Namely, government is compelled to use fair procedures (giving notice of a violation, an opportunity to be heard, and a decision in a case provided by a neutral decision maker) before depriving a citizen of their life, liberty, or property. **Substantive due process** refers to the laws themselves and whether they are fair and reasonable. Thus, even if a law passes the test of procedural due process, it can be unconstitutional if it is "unreasonable" in light of Constitutional protections.

THE BILL OF RIGHTS: INCORPORATION

Originally, the Bill of Rights only applied to the federal government. However, through a process known as **incorporation**, the Supreme Court has used the due process clause of the 14th Amendment – which declares that no *state* can "deprive any person of life, liberty, or property, without due process of law" – to extend Constitutional protections from the federal level to the state level as well. As discussed on the previous page, in order to have legal standing, a state law would have to have not just procedural due process but also substantive – that is, being in accordance with the Constitution. The Supreme Court incorporates selectively, and not all of the amendments have been incorporated yet.

The Bill of Rights and its evolution through the courts has both profoundly shaped American society and served as a reflection of how that society has evolved. In the following pages we will consider some of the individual amendments in this light.

WAIT, SO DOES THAT MEAN THE STATE CAN FORCE ME TO LET SOLDIERS LIVE IN MY HOUSE? I MEAN, SINCE IT HASN'T BEEN INCORPORATED?
HARD TO IMAGINE THAT HAPPENING BUT, YES, I SUPPOSE SO.
AT LEAST, THEY COULD UNLESS YOU SUED AND IT MADE ITS WAY TO THE SUPREME COURT.
INCORPORATED guarantees
FREE EXERCISE OF RELIGION
Freedom of press and assembly
Protection against double jeopardy
Right to keep + bear arms
freedom of speech
PROTECTION AGAINST CRUEL + UNUSUAL PUNISHMENT
Privilege against self-incrimination
FREEDOM FROM QUARTERING OF SOLDIERS
Freedom from unreasonable search and seizure
Warrant requirements
Right to indictment by a grand jury
JURY TRIAL IN CIVIL CASES
Protection against excessive fines
NOT [ENTIRELY] INCORPORATED guarantees

FIRST AMENDMENT: FREEDOM OF RELIGION

The 1st Amendment is just 45 words long but packs the potential for an enormous number of protections. The section regarding religion is very terse, stating, "Congress shall make no law respecting an establishment of religion, or prohibiting the free exercise thereof." From this, the amendment has been divided into its two parts: the "**Establishment Clause**" and the "**Free Exercise Clause**," both of which have had profound consequences in how Americans practice their faith, or absence of. The Establishment Clause keeps the government from establishing an official religion or from making laws that favor one religion over another. The Free Exercise Clause, in contrast, allows Americans protection to believe what they wish and to practice their religion, within certain boundaries.

FREEDOM OF RELIGION: THE LEMON TEST

Pennsylvania and Rhode Island had enacted statutes that extended extra pay to teachers in religious schools, to mirror payment to teachers at public schools, as long as the teachers were teaching non-religious subjects. The practice was challenged in the late 1960's and found unconstitutional by the Supreme Court. In *Lemon v. Kurtzman* (1970), the Court provided a three-part test for analyzing a case in light of the Establishment Clause – thereafter known as the "Lemon Test":

1) the statute must have a secular legislative purpose;
2) its principal or primary effect must be one that neither advances nor inhibits religion; and
3) the statute must not foster "an excessive government entanglement with religion."

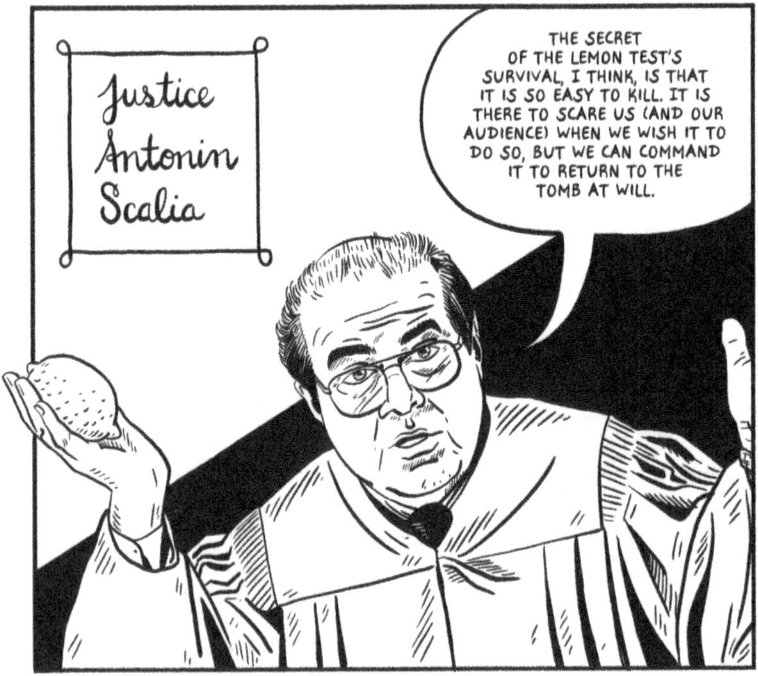

The practice of paying non-public school teachers was found to violate the third part of the test. Justice Scalia (who served on the Court from 1986-2016) criticized the Lemon Test as being too easy to use when it suited a case and ignore when it didn't.

FIRST AMENDMENT: FREEDOM OF SPEECH

Americans hold dear their ability to speak their mind and to express themselves in many forms. Still, the government can create reasonable restrictions on speech. Words used in order to inflict injury on another person or to inspire them to acts of violence ("**fighting words**") are not protected. **Libel** (written defamation of another person) is also not allowed. However, it is much harder to prosecute someone for libel if the person they are criticizing is a public official or public figure. As determined by the landmark Supreme Court case *New York Times Co. v. Sullivan* (1964), in order to successfully prosecute, it would have to be proved that the person accused was acting with "actual malice," meaning that they knew a statement was false and printed it anyway. Such cases are very hard to win, a fact that some tabloid newspapers take full advantage of.

FIRST AMENDMENT: FREEDOM OF ASSEMBLY

The right to freedom of speech means much less if people don't have the ability to publicly express their beliefs – thus the right to freedom of assembly. While Americans have a Constitutional right to protest and gather for positive demonstrations, that right is not without restrictions. It has been determined that "reasonable" restrictions on "assemblies" include:

- **time:** you can't block the streets of, say, Times Square during rush hour;
- **place:** public places with very specific functions such as jailhouses and military bases are off limits; and
- **manner:** you can't use an assembly to advocate or incite violence.

Generally, police are not supposed to intervene unless there is a "clear and present danger of riot, disorder, or interference with traffic on public streets, or other immediate threat to public safety or order." Of course, how the government responds to an assembly can vary greatly among states, cities, neighborhoods, and, particularly, by how the police force is trained.

SECOND AMENDMENT: RIGHT TO KEEP AND BEAR ARMS

One of the most strongly-debated amendments to the Constitution is the 2nd, which states that: "A well regulated militia being necessary to the security of a free State, the right of the People to keep and bear arms shall not be infringed." The Founders wanted to ensure that localities had the ability to protect themselves from both internal and external threats through the use of **state militias** – armed citizens who could be assembled when the need arose. While the militia system of defense is officially no longer in use, gun rights advocates continue to cite the 2nd Amendment in their fight against gun restrictions. We will address the gun debate in the final section of this book.

FOURTH AMENDMENT: SEARCH AND SEIZURE

In the United States, our bodies, properties, and homes are supposed to be safe from random searches by the police or government agents. To protect Americans from unreasonable searches and seizures, the 4th Amendment requires that police obtain a valid **search warrant** (a court order that authorizes them to conduct a search), which describes precisely "the place to be searched, and the persons or things to be seized." Warrants must be issued only when there is **probable cause** or reasonable grounds for believing that a law has been broken. Until the landmark Supreme Court case of *Mapp v. Ohio* in 1961, evidence obtained unconstitutionally or illegally could be used in trial at the state level (it had been prohibited at the federal level since 1911). *Mapp* established the **exclusionary rule**, which stated that such evidence had to be excluded from trial evidence.

FIFTH AMENDMENT: SELF-INCRIMINATION AND DOUBLE JEOPARDY

The 5th Amendment offers additional protections for those accused or suspected of a crime. In addition to prohibiting an individual being tried for the same crime twice – **double jeopardy** – it also states that people cannot be forced or coerced into being a witness against themselves. When a person refuses to answer questions that may incriminate them, they may say that they "plead the 5th." Through the Supreme Court, that protection was extended in scope from just criminal trials to other forms of interrogation such as legislative investigations and, most controversially, police interrogations. However, for a long time there was no clear standard for how the right would be enforced when police questioned suspects. It was the Supreme Court case, *Miranda v. Arizona* (1966) that gave guidance, requiring that officers remind individuals of their constitutional right to remain silent – thereafter known as their **Miranda Rights** – by giving a Miranda Warning.

SIXTH AMENDMENT: RIGHT TO COUNSEL

The right for a person accused of a crime to have a lawyer, part of the 6th Amendment, has been interpreted differently over the years. The **Federal Crimes Act** (1790) required the courts to provide counsel only in capital cases (those punishable by death). In 1938, this was extended to all federal criminal proceedings but was not yet incorporated to the states. This changed when in 1963 a poor man named Clarence Earl Gideon was on trial for breaking and entering, and his request for an attorney was denied. He did his best to represent himself but lost his case. During his time in prison, he petitioned the Florida Supreme Court, arguing that his lack of an attorney was a violation of his constitutional right to counsel. When that petition was denied, Gideon submitted a petition to the federal Supreme Court, which sided with him.

A RIGHT TO PRIVACY

The right to privacy is central to American values but is not mentioned explicitly in the Constitution. Rather, the Supreme Court, though various rulings, has determined that it exists via the interpretation of other protections extended through the Bill of Rights. The 5th Amendment's protection against self-incrimination, for example, implies that we have the right to privacy of information about ourselves. The 1st Amendment implies a right to privacy of beliefs. It was the right to privacy stemming from the due process clause of the 14th Amendment that provided the basis for the Supreme Court's decision in *Roe. v. Wade* (1973) that protected a woman's right to have an abortion.

PART II: THE BALANCE OF POWER

The structure of the government of the United States was carefully crafted to provide a balance of power between the presidency, judiciary, and legislative branches. Although the media has sometimes been called the "fourth branch" of government, we will look into that in more detail in Part III, which covers "politics from the ground up." The structure of Native American politics and its relationship to the federal government is also part of this balance of power, although it often gets overlooked. In this section, we'll address questions like:

THE PRESIDENCY

For much of American history, Congress held a disproportionate share of power. This shifted in the 1930's with the presidency of Franklin D. Roosevelt, who served four terms as president (it wasn't until the ratification of the 22nd Amendment in 1951 that presidents were limited to two terms). His leadership during WWII enhanced presidential war powers, and his enactment of the New Deal as a response to the Great Depression reflected a growth in the legislative powers of the office of president. The war powers of the president expanded again during the Vietnam War under Johnson, and during the War on Terror under George W. Bush. Of course, many people have been critical of this expansion of power. Arthur Schlesinger, in his 1973 book, *The Imperial Presidency,* argued that it was concerning. Interest in his work was revived after the presidential actions following the attacks of 9/11.

"THE ANSWER TO THE RUNAWAY PRESIDENCY IS NOT THE MESSENGER-BOY PRESIDENCY. THE AMERICAN DEMOCRACY MUST DISCOVER A MIDDLE GROUND BETWEEN MAKING THE PRESIDENT A CZAR AND MAKING HIM A PUPPET."
-ARTHUR SCHLESINGER-

ELECTING THE PRESIDENT: THE ELECTORAL COLLEGE

The concept of **majority rule** is foundational to the democratic process. In every state and local election in the United States, the candidate with the most votes is declared the winner. However, this is not the case for one office: the presidency.

When voters cast their ballots for president, they are not voting for the presidential candidate of their choice. Rather, they are voting for a slate of electors – the **electoral college** – who are chosen by the state's Democratic or Republican parties. Each state receives one elector for each senator (two total) and additional electors equal to the state's number of representatives in the House of Representatives (a number that varies with, and is proportional to, their population). Washington DC receives three electors, although it does not have representation in Congress.

PEOPLE ARE ALWAYS WHINING ABOUT THE ELECTORAL COLLEGE. JUST SORE LOSERS, IF YOU ASK ME.
COME ON! HILLARY CLINTON WON THE POPULAR VOTE BY 2.9 MILLION VOTES AND GORE HAD HALF A MILLION MORE THAN BUSH!
SURE, BUT I BET YOU WEREN'T COMPLAINING WHEN DEMOCRATS WON.
THE LAST THREE TIMES IN HISTORY IT HAS HAPPENED, IT WAS A DEMOCRAT WHO WON THE POPULAR VOTE BUT LOST THE ELECTION!

ARGUMENTS IN FAVOR OF THE ELECTORAL COLLEGE

There have been five elections in American history where a candidate won the popular vote (meaning, they received the majority of votes) but lost the electoral vote: 1824, 1876, 1888, 2000, and 2016. After two in such a short period of time, it isn't surprising that people around the world tried to understand what the advantages of such a system could be. When the Constitution was written, the electoral college represented a compromise between large and small states as well as for those delegates who were wary of direct election by popular vote. It can ensure that the president has broad approval, not just the support of the most populous cities.

POWERS OF THE PRESIDENT

When Donald Trump took the office of president, he outlined an ambitious agenda for his first 100 days, as many presidents do. Both supporters and opponents wondered what would be in his power to accomplish. Indeed, walking the line between voter expectations, political agendas, and presidential power is one of the biggest challenges for a president. It is worth noting that when we think of presidential power, we cannot only consider it in terms of specifically enumerated powers or the most commonly understood implied powers. Richard E. Neustadt argued, in his seminal study of the presidency, that we must also think of it in terms of the ability to influence and persuade. For example, when President Trump tweets about a particular company and its stock either rises or declines in response, that is power, even though it doesn't arise from the Constitution.

PRESIDENTIAL POWERS: MILITARY

The United States maintains the largest military in the world (Russia and China are the other contenders), and the president is constitutionally vested as the **Commander-in-Chief**, or top officer of that military force. One of the biggest controversies over this power is in the president's ability to utilize the military without a Congressional declaration of war. For example, Presidents Lyndon Johnson and Richard Nixon waged the Vietnam War without it ever being officially declared by Congress. Congress tried to reign in this power with the **War Powers Act** (1973), which required the president to notify Congress within 48 hours of sending troops into a conflict and to not keep troops engaged for more than 60 days (and an additional 30-day withdrawal period) without congressional approval. However, the Act generally has been ignored by presidents, and there has not been a formal declaration of war since WWII.

PRESIDENTIAL POWERS: LEGISLATIVE

In theory, the legislative powers of the president as outlined in the Constitution are fairly small, in order to preserve the balance of power between the different branches of government. The president is allowed to give a yearly **State of the Union** address before Congress "to recommend to their consideration such measures as he shall judge necessary and expedient." The State of the Union has become an important way for the president to announce their policy agenda not just to Congress but to the American public. The president can then put pressure on members of Congress to put forth legislation that would help fulfill that agenda. More critically, the president has the ability to use the **presidential veto** to kill legislation sent to their desk from Congress. Bills that are vetoed can be overridden by a two-thirds vote from Congress, but gaining enough votes to do so can be difficult, increasing the power of the veto.

PRESIDENTIAL POWERS: EXECUTIVE ORDERS

A president can also legislate through the use of executive orders and presidential directives. Unilateral action through the issuance of executive orders is a tool that has been used by many presidents to a greater or lesser degree. Franklin D. Roosevelt issued 3,721 executive orders during his presidency. It was his executive order 9066, signed in 1942, that cleared the way for creating internment camps for Japanese Americans during WWII. Since a numbering system began in the 1930's, over 13,000 have been issued. Sometimes the orders are mundane, such as creating a public holiday. Other times they attempt to circumvent Congress to push forward an agenda that would otherwise be difficult to pass. Executive orders have the force of law, as long as they are based on power vested in the president by the Constitution or delegated to the president by Congress.

[redacted]

[redacted]

EXECUTIVE ORDERS: LIMITS

The power that a president can wield through the issuance of executive orders is not unlimited. The judiciary has the power to rule them unlawful. President Trump's executive order suspending the entry of immigrants from predominantly Muslim nations and all refugees, issued just one week into his presidency in 2017, was met with a restraining order that was later upheld by the United States Court of Appeals for the Ninth Circuit. Congress can also refuse to fund an order, as was the case when President Obama issued an executive order to close the prison at Guantánamo Bay, Cuba. A third check on executive orders is the Department of Justice's Office of Legal Counsel, whose job it is to review proposed executive orders for form and legality. Of course, unpopular orders also can face a backlash from voters, which can create political pressure.

PRESIDENTIAL DIRECTIVES

A president also has the authority to issue a **presidential directive** (also known as a **presidential decision directive**), under the advice and counsel of the National Security Administration. Accordingly, they tend to be concerned with matters of national security. What is the difference between an executive order and a presidential directive? For one, directives can be more secretive since, unlike executive orders, they are not required to be made public through posting in the *Federal Register*. For example, controversy flared in 2005 when media reports revealed that three years earlier President George W. Bush had passed a secret executive order authorizing the National Security Agency to eavesdrop without a warrant on phone calls made by US citizens and others living in the United States. Directives need not always be secret, but since they concern national security, full details are rarely revealed.

"EVEN THOUGH YOU HEAR THE WORDS, 'DOMESTIC SPYING,' THESE ARE NOT PHONE CALLS WITHIN THE UNITED STATES. THIS IS A PHONE CALL OF AN AL-QAEDA, KNOWN AL-QAEDA SUSPECT, MAKING A PHONE CALL INTO THE UNITED STATES."
IT'S A DIFFERENT KIND OF WAR WITH A DIFFERENT KIND OF ENEMY. IF THEY'RE MAKING PHONE CALLS INTO THE UNITED STATES, WE NEED TO KNOW WHY – TO PROTECT YOU.

PRESIDENTIAL POWERS: DIPLOMATIC

So far we haven't considered the international political environment much, but the United States doesn't exist in a vacuum, and one of the president's key roles is as the head of state. Formally, the president has the constitutional power to make treaties with other nations, as long as they can get a two-thirds vote of support in the Senate. That power has been expanded through the use of executive agreements – made between two or more heads of state – that skirt the need for Senate consent. The **General Agreement on Tariffs and Trade (GATT)**, a post-WWII agreement to reduce barriers to trade among 23 nations, was an executive agreement.

The type of rhetoric that different presidents use when taking on world challenges tends to reflect both their personal style and how they interpret the state of critical world affairs.

"THREATS FROM NORTH KOREA WILL BE MET WITH FIRE, FURY, AND FRANKLY POWER THE LIKES OF WHICH THIS WORLD HAS NEVER SEEN BEFORE."
TRUMP
"TODAY'S NUCLEAR TEST, A FLAGRANT VIOLATION OF MULTIPLE UN SECURITY COUNCIL RESOLUTIONS, MAKES CLEAR NORTH KOREA'S DISREGARD FOR INTERNATIONAL NORMS AND STANDARDS FOR BEHAVIOR AND DEMONSTRATES IT HAS NO INTEREST IN BEING A RESPONSIBLE MEMBER OF THE INTERNATIONAL COMMUNITY."
OBAMA
"MULTILATERAL DIPLOMACY IS THE BEST WAY TO PEACEFULLY SOLVE THE NUCLEAR ISSUE WITH NORTH KOREA."
BUSH
"IF NORTH KOREA DEVELOPED AND USED AN ATOMIC WEAPON, WE WOULD QUICKLY AND OVERWHELMINGLY RETALIATE. IT WOULD MEAN THE END OF THEIR COUNTRY AS THEY KNOW IT."
CLINTON

PRESIDENTIAL POWERS: APPOINTMENT

While the appointment of a Supreme Court justice captures center stage because it is a lifetime appointment that grants a lot of power of constitutional interpretation, the president is able to nominate individuals for appointment to a broad array of offices beyond the Court. This covers all officers of the United States (including ambassadors, public ministers, and consuls). However, the Constitution says that certain appointments must be confirmed by the Senate. Currently, between 1,200 and 1,400 positions require confirmation. Presidents also have a constitutional power to make appointments during a Senate recess to bypass Senate approval. Different presidents have taken advantage of this power to varying extents: at 232 recess appointments, Ronald Reagan made the most of this power; Bill Clinton made 139, George W. Bush 171, and Barack Obama just 32.

THE PRESIDENCY: IMPEACHMENT AND REMOVAL FROM OFFICE

It is not uncommon for the question of **impeachment** of a president to be bandied about by critics. An impeachment does not necessarily mean a removal from office – as the impeachment (and subsequent acquittal) of former presidents Bill Clinton (1993–2001) and Andrew Jackson (1829–37) attests. The Constitution permits the removal of a president from office after the impeachment *and* conviction for crimes including "Treason, Bribery, or other High Crimes and Misdemeanors." President Richard Nixon (1969–74) came close with the **Watergate** scandal, in which he was impeached for (among other charges) obstruction of justice, abuse of power, and criminal cover up, but he resigned before he could be convicted.

THE PRESIDENCY: SUCCESSION

The 25th Amendment describes the process of succession, should the president die, resign, be removed from office, or become unable to fulfill their duties due to impairment. The president can invoke it in order to allow for a temporary transfer of power when, say, they are under sedation for surgery (as did George W. Bush for about two hours when he was undergoing a colonoscopy in 2002). Otherwise, it can be invoked by the vice president and a majority of the members of the cabinet by submitting a declaration to Congress that the president is unfit. Once submitted, the vice president immediately assumes power. The president can contest the declaration to regain power, and, if that happens, Congress has 21 days to reach a two-thirds majority vote in favor of declaring the president unable to discharge the powers and duties of their office.

THE VICE PRESIDENT

Considering the fact that the vice president is just a heartbeat away from the presidency, the position is vested with surprisingly little power. They are to take over the presidency if the president dies, resigns or is incapacitated – which has occurred 9 times in American history. Further, as president of the Senate, the vice president can cast a tie-breaking vote when it is evenly divided.

A presidential candidate selects a particular person to act as their vice presidential running mate for a number of reasons, but most of them are electorally strategic. Picking someone from a swing state can help to win the state. If a presidential candidate is seen as lacking experience in some way, the selection of someone with a background in that area can alleviate concerns. Of course, it is important to note that "chemistry" between the two is key, as, once they take office, the vice president becomes a crucial advisor and confidant of the president.

@VP
Happy 55th, Barack! A brother to me, a best friend forever.
JOE
BARACK

THE CABINET

The Constitution only vaguely references the existence of a cabinet as, while the founders felt that the president would want a council of advisors, they weren't able to agree on exactly how it would be formed. Article II, Section 2 says that the president may "require the opinion, in writing, of the principal officer in each of the executive departments, upon any subject relating to the duties of their respective offices." Still, every president since George Washington has made use of a cabinet, and currently it consists of the vice president and 15 members, who must be confirmed by the Senate and who form the line of succession, should the president be unable to perform their duties. Presidents have the discretion to name additional cabinet members who need not be confirmed.

THE EXECUTIVE OFFICE OF THE PRESIDENT

During the presidency of Franklin D. Roosevelt, the Executive Office of the President was created to provide support for running the complex array of federal departments and agencies by providing the president with information and expert advice. One of the most important offices is the **Office of Management and Budget**, which helps the president exert control over those departments and agencies by providing administrative and budgetary oversight. Its budget work is different from, and can clash with, the **Congressional Budget Office**, which is a part of the legislative branch tasked with providing nonpartisan budget analysis to Congress.

CONGRESS'S ROLE IN THE BALANCE OF POWER

While the election of the president is separated from the voter by the electoral college, it is the **bicameral** Congress (divided into two parts – the Senate and the House of Representatives) that is supposed to best express the voice of the average American, as each member's primary responsibility is to represent the needs and hopes of their **constituency** (the residents of the area in which they are elected). Each state is allocated 2 senators, regardless of its size. The 435 members of the House of Representatives are allocated to each state according to its population, as it stands at the time of the census, which is conducted every 10 years (with each state guaranteed at least one representative). Together, the House and Senate comprise the legislative branch of government, and any **bill** (proposed law) has to be agreed upon by both chambers before it can be signed into law.

CONSTITUTIONAL POWERS

Congress has 17 powers enumerated in the Constitution. They include:

ISSUE COPYRIGHTS & PATENTS
DEFINE + punish PIRACY
Create courts below the Supreme Court
DECLARE WAR and RAISE ARMIES
Provide a Navy
MAKE ALL necessary LAWS
THE WHITE HOUSE

CONGRESSIONAL OVERSIGHT

Congress is also important in the balance of power, in that it provides **oversight** over the executive branch. Congress can launch investigations and hearings with the goal of ensuring that the executive (and the agencies of the bureaucracy controlled by it) is doing its job and following the law. Oversight is formally conducted in the House of Representatives through the **Oversight and Government Reform Committee** and in the Senate through the **Homeland Security and Governmental Affairs Committee**. This investigatory role is not expressly given by the Constitution. Rather, it is an implied power. Some express powers of Congress include the power to remove a president or judge from office through impeachment, and to confirm or deny the president's nominees for political appointments. Oversight can also be conducted through legislative committees, which may enact laws to curb the powers of certain agencies, and through **appropriation** – the allocation of resources to government and bureaucratic departments. Congressional oversight hasn't been without controversy, as in the hearings of Senator McCarthy's House Un-American Activities Committee.

PARTY AND POWER IN CONGRESS

While the level of oversight conducted by Congress is supposed to be **bipartisan** and cooperative between parties, it is no secret that when the **majority party** (the party with the most seats) in either the House or Senate is different from that which holds the executive, it tends to scrutinize the executive branch more. In general, political parties play a huge role in how Congress is run. The majority party gets the most influential roles: the Speaker of the House and the Senate majority leader. It also decides who chairs the committees and subcommittees, and it can decide the legislative agenda (what legislation will be considered and when). Because a bill can only become law when both the House and Senate agree on it, a **divided Congress** – one in which the majority party is different for the House and Senate – can make passing legislation much more challenging.

CONGRESSIONAL ELECTIONS

There are constitutional restrictions on who can run for Congress. Members of the House of Representatives must be at least 25 years old and have been a citizen for 7 years. Senators must be at least 30 and a citizen for 9 years. While the 115th Congress was one of the most diverse in history, women and minorities still only made up about 20% of elected officials. **Incumbents** (those who already hold the elected office being contested) have a strong advantage, and 98% of incumbents won re-election in the 2017 elections. There are no limits to the number of terms that a politician can serve in the House or Senate. John Dingell, a Democrat representing Michigan in the House, served for 59 years, the longest of any congressperson to date.

CAMPAIGN FINANCE

Money plays a strong role in who runs for Congress and who gets elected. According to the Center for Responsive Politics, the average cost of running for Senate in 2016 was $10.4 million, up $1.8 million from the election cycle just two years earlier. The amount spent on House campaigns, in contrast, was much less: about $1.3 million. However, these numbers just include the money spent directly by a campaign and don't account for the often huge sums of money spent by political interest groups and **super PACs** (an organization that pools unlimited contributions from various groups, individuals, and corporations and spends that money to influence elections). Campaign finance will be explored in greater detail in the final section of this book.

I HEARD THAT CLINTON AND TRUMP SPENT OVER A BILLION DOLLARS ON THEIR CAMPAIGNS. THAT IS JUST INSANE.
THAT'S JUST WHAT THEY SPENT THEMSELVES. IF YOU COUNT THE SPENDING OF OTHER GROUPS, IT'S CLOSER TO $2.4 BILLION.
IT GETS CRAZIER. IF YOU COUNT THE FREE AIRTIME ON TV, WHICH WAS WORTH ABOUT $8 BILLION, IT COST OVER $10 BILLION. WHERE DOES IT ALL GO? WHERE DID IT ALL COME FROM?
ALL THAT MONEY AND IT DIDN'T CHANGE MY OPINION ONE BIT. TOTAL WASTE.

REDISTRICTING, REAPPORTIONMENT, AND GERRYMANDERING

The House of Representatives has 435 members who are divided among the states in a process known as **reapportionment**; the number a state is allocated is proportionate to its population as determined by the census, which occurs every 10 years. Each representative represents a district, which currently encompasses 711,000 people. After each census, state legislatures with more than one district engage in **redistricting**, in which the boundaries of each district are redrawn. Redistricting is an intensely political process, as the way that districts are drawn can have deep consequences for how power is distributed. When district lines are drawn in such a way as to intentionally benefit one group, it is known as gerrymandering. **Racial gerrymandering** occurs when they are drawn in order to benefit or disadvantage a racial group.

HOW CONGRESS WORKS: THE COMMITTEE SYSTEM

The complexity of the legislative work involved in Congress necessitates a strong organizational structure, as up to 10,000 bills can be introduced over a two-year period. In order to divide up the work, Congress is split into **standing committees** (permanent committees that specialize in a subject area), **special** or **select committees** (formed for a limited period to perform a particular study or investigation), and **joint committees** (which do work similar to select committees but include members from both the House and Senate). The committees can be in charge of budgeting, setting rules about how governmental programs are run, appropriating money for programs, raising revenue, reconciling differences between House and Senate bills, and providing oversight.

HOW A BILL BECOMES A LAW

While many bills are introduced, as few as 4% make their way to becoming law. The path for a bill is slightly different between the House and Senate but, generally: bills are introduced; they go to committee for mark up; to the floor for debate, reconciliation, and passage; and then to the president to be signed into law. This path sounds deceptively simple but, in reality, there are many ways for bills to be "killed" before they ever reach the White House for signing. For one, once a bill goes to the appropriate committee, there is a limited amount of time for it to be acted upon before it "dies." Because of the large volume of bills introduced – 10,768 between January 2015 and January 2017 – the bills that get attention are usually those with a lot of political muscle behind them.

LOBBYING CONGRESS

In the US, there are over 11,000 registered **lobbyists** – people engaged in activities with the express intent of influencing governmental policymakers. Lobbyists may come from (or be hired by) interest groups representing businesses, nonprofits, local-level constituents, or just about any part of society. Lobbying can be direct or indirect. Direct lobbying involves visits with officials or their staff, making phone calls, and writing letters or emails. Indirect lobbying is more about efforts to shape the opinions of the public, and thus creating political influence, through grassroots techniques. Vast sums of money are poured into lobbying efforts, with a yearly reported average of close to $2.5 billion. We'll explore interest groups in greater depth later in the book.

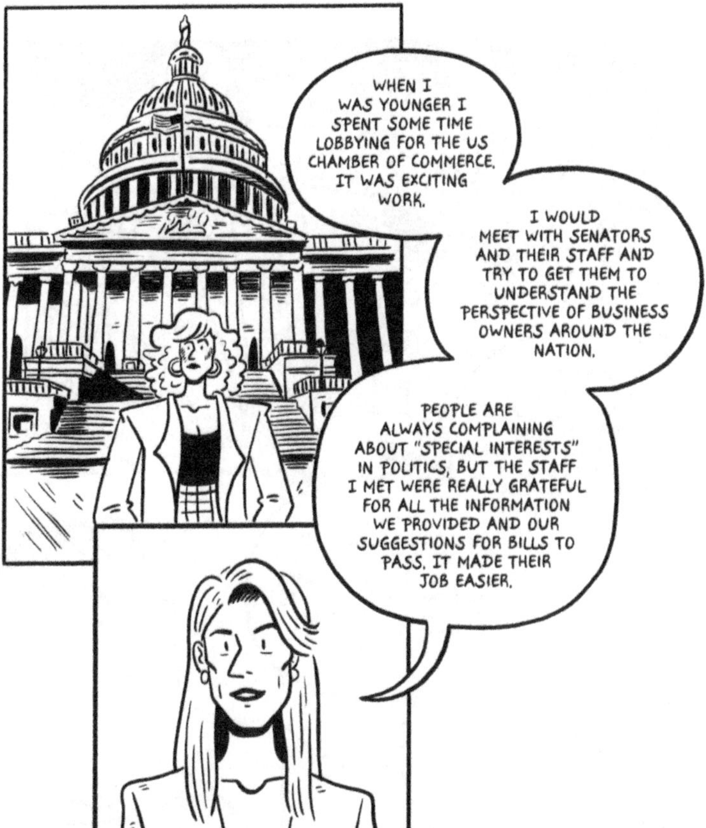

THE JUDICIARY'S ROLE IN THE BALANCE OF POWER

Our lives are directly and constantly affected by the rule of law. Clear, impartial, and evenly enforced laws give a democratic society the predictability it needs to function. In the US, the judiciary is charged with enforcing local, state, and federal laws and interpreting whether those laws are constitutional. Laws can be **substantive** (defining what we can and cannot do) or **procedural** (establishing how the law is applied and enforced). When an individual engages in an action prohibited by the government, that violation is called a **crime** and they are subject to **criminal law**. When an individual is accused of a harmful action against another person (failing to fulfill a contract, for example), they are subject to **civil law** and the violation is called a **tort**. Some actions can be subject to both types of law.

IT WASN'T UNTIL THE OJ SIMPSON TRIALS THAT I UNDERSTOOD THE DIFFERENCE BETWEEN CIVIL AND CRIMINAL LAW AND HOW YOU CAN BE TRIED TWICE FOR THE SAME CRIME.
OJ WAS ACCUSED OF MURDERING HIS WIFE. AT HIS CRIMINAL TRIAL, THEY SAID THAT THERE WASN'T ENOUGH EVIDENCE TO LOCK HIM UP – HIS HAND COULDN'T FIT INTO THE MURDER GLOVE.
BUT HE WAS CONVICTED AT THE CIVIL TRIAL. THE CIVIL COURT CAN'T PUT A PERSON IN PRISON, BUT IT DID ORDER HIM TO PAY A BUNCH OF MONEY.

THE HISTORY OF THE JUDICIARY

The decision to create an independent judiciary was a novel experiment at the time the Constitution was written. The Constitution doesn't give a lot of detail about how the courts can act as a check to the other branches of government. It states simply: "The judicial Power of the United States, shall be vested in one supreme Court, and in such inferior Courts as the Congress may from time to time ordain and establish." It goes on to describe the reason judges can be fired, their compensation, the jurisdictions of federal courts, and the way in which someone can be tried for treason. The **Judiciary Act of 1789**, adopted during the first session of the first US Congress, established the structure of the judicial branch. However, it wasn't until *Marbury v. Madison (1803)* that the courts' place in the balance of power was truly established, as it set the precedent for **judicial review**, where courts can review actions of the executive and legislative branches and potentially declare them invalid or unconstitutional.

THE STRUCTURE OF THE COURTS

The legal structure in the US is divided into state and federal courts. Which court hears which case is determined by a court's **jurisdiction**: the geographic region or type of legal cases upon which it has legal authority to rule. There are certain types of cases upon which a court has **original jurisdiction** (the authority to hear a case first), and others where it has **appellate jurisdiction** (the authority to review decisions made by lower courts). State courts have original jurisdiction over most civil and criminal cases in which everyday citizens are involved. Federal courts have original jurisdiction over cases involving federal law, such as cases where the US itself is a party, cases involving a constitutional violation, disputes between citizens of different states where the amount involved exceeds $75,0000, cases involving Native Americans, and bankruptcy and antitrust laws.

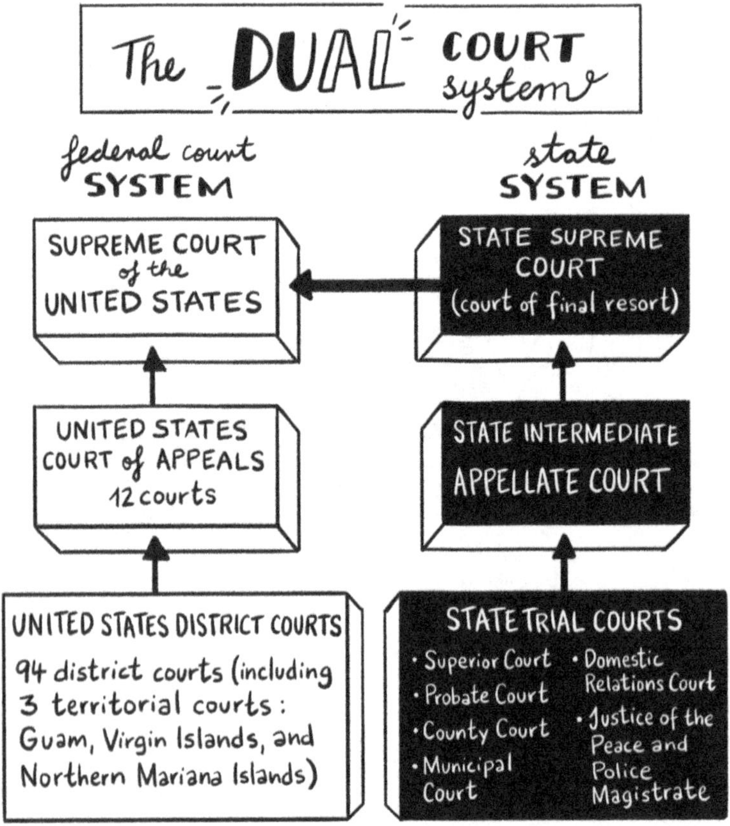

THE SUPREME COURT

The Supreme Court is the highest court in the US. Justices serve a lifetime term, which is supposed to reduce their ability to be influenced by the politics of the moment in that they won't be tempted to make decisions based on a desire to be re-elected. However, in practice, political parties see the ability to nominate a justice seen as "liberal" or "conservative" as a way of ensuring the the Constitution will be interpreted in accordance with their political ideology. Nominations for a new Supreme Court justice are made by the president and confirmed by the Senate.

The Supreme Court receives about 7,000 requests for hearings a year, but typically hears only 80 and decides on another 50 or so without needing to hear arguments in person.

THE SUPREME COURT: ORIGINALISM

One of the greatest debates surrounding Constitutional interpretation is how exactly a modern society should interpret a 230-year-old document. One way is originalism, in which the meaning of the Constitution is considered fixed at the time it was written, such that Supreme Court rulings should be based on interpretations of **original intent** or **original meaning**. Original intent is less common, seeking to interpret the Constitution according to the intent of the framers themselves. Original meaning focuses more directly on language, taking the view that, while circumstances may change, we cannot reinterpret the words in the Constitution to fit. Originalism is usually associated with more politically conservative judges. It has been critiqued by scholars such as Colombia Law Professor Jamal Greene, who argues that African Americans in particular are skeptical of an interpretation that looks backward in time, to a period of American history when they were held in slavery.

ANTONIN SCALIA
"THE CONSTITUTION THAT I INTERPRET AND APPLY IS NOT LIVING BUT DEAD, OR AS I PREFER TO CALL IT, ENDURING. IT MEANS TODAY NOT WHAT CURRENT SOCIETY, MUCH LESS THE COURT, THINKS IT OUGHT TO MEAN, BUT WHAT IT MEANT WHEN IT WAS ADOPTED."
BUT WHAT DOES THAT MEAN FOR AFRICAN AMERICANS? WHEN THE CONSTITUTION WAS ADOPTED, A BLACK PERSON WASN'T EVEN CONSIDERED A FULL PERSON, MUCH LESS A CITIZEN.
JAMAL GREENE
"THE QUESTION IS WHETHER, AND IF SO TO WHAT DEGREE, A TENSION EXISTS BETWEEN AFRICAN-AMERICAN IDENTITY AND ORIGINALISM ... A RACIALLY SENSITIVE CONSTITUTIONALISM MUST ALWAYS HOLD OUT THE POSSIBILITY OF LEGITIMATE DISSENT FROM HISTORY. ORIGINALISM DENIES THAT POSSIBILITY ... "

THE SUPREME COURT: NON-ORIGINALISM

In contrast to the originalist interpretation, non-originalists believe that the Constitution must be interpreted in a way that evolves with American society and culture. There are a number of strains of thought under the "non-originalist" umbrella: such as the **living Constitution** (viewing it as a "living" document in that it changes according to the times) and **moral interpretations** (in which it is read not literally but, overall, as comprising a set of moral principles). Justice Oliver Wendell Holmes, in his 1920 opinion regarding the *State of Missouri v. Holland*, argued that as gifted as the writers of the Constitution were, there was no way they could have foreseen the developments which have occurred in the 200+ years that have passed since its ratification. Cases, therefore, needed to be viewed "in the light of our whole experience." Barack Obama was also a proponent of this view.

"IN NOMINATING A NEW SUPREME COURT JUSTICE, I WILL SEEK SOMEONE WHO UNDERSTANDS THAT JUSTICE ISN'T ABOUT SOME ABSTRACT LEGAL THEORY OR FOOTNOTE IN A CASEBOOK; IT IS ALSO ABOUT HOW OUR LAWS AFFECT THE DAILY REALITIES OF PEOPLE'S LIVES, WHETHER THEY CAN MAKE A LIVING AND CARE FOR THEIR FAMILIES, WHETHER THEY FEEL SAFE IN THEIR HOMES AND WELCOME IN THEIR OWN NATION. I VIEW THAT QUALITY OF EMPATHY, OF UNDERSTANDING AND IDENTIFYING WITH PEOPLE'S HOPES AND STRUGGLES, AS AN ESSENTIAL INGREDIENT FOR ARRIVING AT JUST DECISIONS AND OUTCOMES."

DISTRICT AND APPEALS COURT

Federal courts below the Supreme Court consist of 94 district courts and 12 courts of appeals. Judges for these courts are appointed by the president, confirmed by Senate, and serve for life. Each state (as well as Washington DC and the US territories) has at least one district court, which is able to hear both criminal and civil cases. Most people, when they end up on trial, find themselves in a state court, but federal courts serve an equally important function. Just as a person can be tried in both a civil and criminal court, they can also be tried in federal court for felony charges and found guilty there – even if they weren't found guilty in the state court. It is also in the federal courts where cases related to the constitutionality of laws are tried, making them a key player in the judicial role in the governmental balance of power.

THE FEDERAL BUREAUCRACY

The word "bureaucracy" tends to bring about negative reactions in many Americans, perhaps because it is the federal bureaucracy that has the most direct contact with the average citizen – whether it is at the post office, unemployment office, or in dealing with student loans. There are over 2.8 million federal employees working in the bureaucracy, staffing departments, agencies and sub-agencies, regulatory boards and commissions, and government corporations.

THERE ARE 15 DEPARTMENTS - INCLUDING THE DEPARTMENTS OF DEFENSE, AGRICULTURE, LABOR, TREASURY, AND ENERGY - THE HEADS OF WHICH ARE REPRESENTED IN THE PRESIDENT'S CABINET.
INDEPENDENT AGENCIES
ARE CALLED SUCH NOT BECAUSE THEY ARE NECESSARILY POLITICALLY INDEPENDENT (INDEED, SOME AGENCY HEADS ARE APPOINTED BY THE PRESIDENT) BUT BECAUSE THEY ARE INDEPENDENT FROM THE FEDERAL DEPARTMENTS.
PEACE CORPS
CENTRAL INTELLIGENCE AGENCY
UNITED STATES OF AMERICA
REGULATORY AGENCIES
LIKE THE FOOD AND DRUG ADMINISTRATION SET REGULATIONS INTENDED TO PROTECT THE PUBLIC.
FINALLY, GOVERNMENTAL CORPORATIONS
(SUCH AS THE US POSTAL SERVICE) ARE CREATED TO PROVIDE GOODS OR SERVICES THAT PRIVATE ENTERPRISE MAY NOT FIND PROFITABLE OR APPEALING.

TRIBAL GOVERNMENT

Describing the balance of power in the United States would be incomplete without a discussion of the balance between the US government and Native American tribal governments. The history of the relationship between indigenous and non-indigenous people in the country is fraught, involving genocide and economic, political, and social marginalization. That relationship today remains complicated. According to the last census, there are 5.2 million Native Americans, 22% of whom live on tribal lands. Overall, life on the reservations is challenging: inhabitants face lower health outcomes than the rest of the United States; almost 30% live in poverty; and 40% of the available housing is considered substandard (with families crammed into what housing is available).

TRIBES AS SOVEREIGN NATIONS

Native American tribes are considered sovereign nations, and there are currently 567 federally recognized nations – 229 in Alaska alone. This sovereignty has been bitterly contested. The attempt to take Cherokee tribal lands in the South in the early 1800s initially led to a ruling in *Cherokee Nation v. Georgia* that tribal nations were not foreign nations but "dependent domestic nations," a relationship comparable to that of, in the words of Justice John Marshall, a "ward to its guardian." A year later, that ruling was overturned, a fact that was ignored by President Andrew Jackson (1829–37), who in 1838 forcibly removed the Cherokee. During their relocation at least 4,000 people died, and it became known as the **Trail of Tears**.

"MANY PEOPLE STILL HAVE A HARD TIME TODAY UNDERSTANDING SOVEREIGNTY. WHAT DOES THIS SOVEREIGNTY OF INDIAN NATIONS MEAN? I HAVE A HARD TIME WITH IT TOO BECAUSE WE'RE NOT SOVEREIGN IN THIS NATION. IF WE WERE SOVEREIGN IN THIS NATION WE WOULD NOT HAVE TO DEPEND ON FEDERAL GOVERNMENT DOLLARS. WE WOULD NOT HAVE TO GO TO THE STATE FOR GAMING APPROVALS. WE WOULD BE ABLE TO LIVE INDEPENDENTLY IN OUR OWN NATION, WHICH IS WHAT WE WERE DOING IN 1838 AT THE TIME OF THE REMOVAL."
JOYCE DUGGAN
FORMER PRINCIPAL CHIEF OF THE EASTERN BAND OF CHEROKEE INDIANS

TRIBAL, STATE, AND FEDERAL LAW

Natives are citizens of the United States, as well as the state in which they reside, and their tribe. This was not always the case, as they were only granted citizenship in the US in 1924, with the **Indian Citizenship Act**. Still, at the time, many states enacted laws specifically aimed at preventing them from voting. It wasn't until the Voting Rights Act (1965) that those barriers were struck down. Voting rights is just one way in which tribal, state, and federal law have been in tension over the years. On the reservation, tribal law is the law of the land, but Native American citizens are still subject to state and federal law. Under the **Major Crimes Act** (1885), most felony offenses such as murder, incest, and serious assault are the jurisdiction of federal courts. The **Assimilative Crimes Act** (1825) made any remaining crimes that were contained in state code (ones where there is no federal statute for the category of offense) a federal crime as well. Essentially, tribal court maintains authority over crimes that are not already covered by state or federal code.

SO, IF I COMMIT A CRIME ON A RESERVATION, DO I HAVE TO GO TO TRIBAL COURT?
PROBABLY NOT. TRIBAL LAW ONLY APPLIES TO INDIANS, UNLESS IT IS A CASE OF, SAY, NON-FELONY DOMESTIC VIOLENCE OR YOU DO SOMETHING TO ASSAULT THE HEALTH AND WELFARE OF THE TRIBE.
HUH. HAS IT ALWAYS BEEN THAT WAY?
NO. TRIBAL COURTS USED TO HAVE MUCH MORE POWER. THAT CHANGED IN 1978 AFTER THE SUPREME COURT RULED IN FAVOR OF A NON-INDIAN MAN WHO DIDN'T FEEL HE SHOULD BE TRIED IN TRIBAL COURT FOR A CRIME HE COMMITTED ON A RESERVATION.

FEDERAL INDIAN TRUST RESPONSIBILITY

It is no understatement to say that the US federal government has taken a paternalistic stance towards Native Americans, stemming from a historical belief that Native American culture was inferior and needed to be reformed (the extensive forced re-education of Native people to white culture being just one example in a long history of actions taken based on this belief). The Federal Indian Trust Responsibility was first articulated in *Cherokee Nation v. Georgia*, but most clearly stated in *Seminole Nation v. United States* (1942): that the US "has charged itself with moral obligations of the highest responsibility and trust" towards Native tribes. Practically, it means that the federal government is charged with both providing support to tribes to improve their quality of life, and holding tribal land in trust - whatever a tribe wishes to do with their land must be approved by the US government. How this responsibility has been discharged has changed over time and has often been controversial among the tribes.

BUREAU OF INDIAN AFFAIRS

In 1824 the Bureau of Indian Affairs (BIA) was formed. Originally it was part of the Department of War, which reflected its view of the Native population as a barrier to westward expansion; it was shifted in 1849 to the Department of the Interior, where it exists today. It was the BIA that implemented the decision to send Native children to boarding schools. Today, the mission of the BIA is to "enhance the quality of life, to promote economic opportunity, and to carry out the responsibility to protect and improve the trust assets of American Indians, Indian tribes, and Alaska Natives."

TRIBAL TERMINATION

In the 1940's, in a continued effort to assimilate Native Americans, the federal government began the policy of "terminating" tribes, ending their federal recognition as tribal entities and ending the federal land trust policy. The land of tribes that were terminated was purchased by the government, and the people were encouraged to move to urban centers. While termination was promoted as a way of improving the lives of natives, it was seen as a way of gaining the resources of tribes whose reservations were found to be located on sites with valuable natural resources. More than 100 tribes were terminated until, in 1970, President Richard Nixon (1969–74) called for an end to the policy. After the policy reversal, many tribes petitioned to regain their status, and 78 were successful.

MAKING PUBLIC POLICY

Thus far, we have examined the structure of government and the laws that govern American society, but it is also necessary to discuss the way in which the US government creates plans of action to solve collective problems - its **public policies**. Generally, public policymaking can be divided up into three categories: foreign policy (how the government will deal with other nations and its place in the international arena); social policy (approaches to increasing the quality of life of the people within US borders); and economic policy (plans for improving the economic health of the nation).

SOME POLICIES ARE REDISTRIBUTIVE, MEANING THAT THEY TAKE RESOURCES FROM ONE GROUP AND GIVE THEM TO ANOTHER, SUCH AS PLACING A HIGHER TAX ON WEALTHIER INDIVIDUALS TO PAY FOR SOCIAL PROGRAMS FOR THE POOR.
DISTRIBUTIVE POLICIES TAKE MONEY FROM ALL TAXPAYERS IN ORDER TO SOLVE A PARTICULAR ISSUE.
$1,000,000
SOCIAL SECURITY PAYMENT
REGULATORY POLICIES AIM TO LIMIT ACTION OR CHANGE BEHAVIOR IN ORDER TO PRODUCE A CERTAIN OUTCOME.
SPEED LIMIT 55

FOREIGN POLICYMAKING

The goal of foreign policy is to improve the security and prosperity of a nation through decisions made on the international stage. During the 18th and 19th centuries, separated by oceans from European and Asian powers, many Americans thought that the best security policy was one of **isolationism**: taking little part in international power struggles. In President George Washington's 1796 farewell address, he warned Americans to avoid permanent alliances with foreign powers. In 1823, President James Monroe warned foreign powers not to meddle in the Western Hemisphere – the basis for what was called the **Monroe Doctrine**. Isolationism was the dominant theme in foreign policy until the 20th century, when technology made oceans a lot less of a barrier to foreign threats, and the world's economic interdependence meant that the US could no longer ignore events abroad. The US entered WWI on the side of Great Britain and France when the Wilson administration decided that America's economic and security interests would be adversely affected by a German victory. In 1941, the US was drawn into WWII after the attack on Pearl Harbor by Japan.

POWER IN THE INTERNATIONAL ARENA

In the international arena, nations utilize political instruments to exert both **soft** and **hard power** in order to wield influence and shape outcomes. Hard power refers to the use of military or economic action, while soft power refers to the many ways to achieve influence socially or culturally – what some refer to as winning over "hearts and minds." **Propaganda** is a type of soft power: leveraging a nation's literature, film, music, advertising, and norms as a persuasive tool for change. **Diplomacy**, the management of relations between nations, typically is another form of soft power in that the goal is to broker resolutions before resorting to the use of force. **Economic sanctions** – trade restrictions enacted to punish another nation – is a form of hard power that has been used on nations such as Burma, Cuba, Iran, Iraq, Côte d'Ivoire, and Syria.

"THE UNITED STATES RESERVES THE RIGHT...
TO ATTACK ANY NATION THAT EITHER HARBORS TERRORISTS OR CONSTITUTES A SERIOUS THREAT TO THE US.
TO ACT UNILATERALLY AGAINST OTHER NATIONS, EVEN IF IT DOES NOT HAVE THE SUPPORT OF ITS ALLIES.
TO USE MASSIVE FORCE AGAINST ITS ENEMIES, INCLUDING NUCLEAR WEAPONS IF NEEDED."

While the majority of the American public agrees that the United States must protect its interests abroad, there is a lot of disagreement over how this should be conducted. The decision to provide military aid during WWII was fraught, and other wars, such as in Vietnam and Korea, were even more controversial. More recently, President George W. Bush (2001–9) asserted that the United States needed to take preemptive action against hostile and threatening states, a policy that came to be known as the **Bush Doctrine**. Part of the Bush doctrine was based on the idea of **preemption**: that the nation may need to take action to stop an immediate and imminent threat. It also could be expressed by waging a **preventative war**, to prevent a sequence of events that could possibly pose a threat later. It was this philosophy that justified his decision to go to war in Iraq in 2003, arguing that there was evidence that the nation had weapons of mass destruction.

COLLECTIVE DEFENSE AGREEMENTS

One tool in maintaining an international balance of power when faced with a threat is the formation of collective defense agreements. The **North Atlantic Treaty** (1949), which formed the **North Atlantic Treaty Organization** (**NATO**), is one of the oldest modern agreements. The 28 signing nations agreed that an attack upon one of them would be considered an attack upon all, and that they would take joint action should a signing nation be threatened. Collective decision making and joint action has a long history: the 1648 Peace of Westphalia and the 1815 Concert of Europe were both examples of agreements that, in part, provided for collective security among European nations. A more modern example is the **League of Nations**, established in 1919–20 (which the United States never joined), which was eventually replaced by the **United Nations** in 1945.

THE FIRST AND ONLY TIME THE MUTUAL PROTECTION WAS INVOKED WAS AFTER THE TERRORIST ATTACKS OF SEPTEMBER 11TH, 2001
OUR MESSAGE TO THE PEOPLE OF THE UNITED STATES IS THAT WE ARE WITH YOU. OUR MESSAGE TO THOSE WHO PERPETRATED THESE UNSPEAKABLE CRIMES IS EQUALLY CLEAR: YOU WILL NOT GET AWAY WITH IT.
EVENTUALLY NATO SENT MILITARY PLANES TO HELP GUARD US AIRSPACE.

TRADE AGREEMENTS

Nations also come together to protect their economic interests. Every nation seeks to be competitive in the global economy, ultimately hoping to export more than they import. Sometimes nations band together regionally to provide each other with preferential trade agreements. The president has usually been granted trade promotion authority (TPA), the ability to "fast track" trade agreements – meaning that Congress cannot amend or filibuster trade agreements, only approve or deny them. That authority was used in negotiating the **North American Free Trade Agreement (NAFTA)**, signed in 1992 under the George H.W. Bush administration and ratified in 1993 during the Clinton administration, which created a free trade zone between Mexico, the United States, and Canada.

"YOU IMPLEMENT THAT MEXICAN TRADE AGREEMENT, WHERE THEY PAY PEOPLE A DOLLAR AN HOUR, HAVE NO HEALTH CARE, NO RETIREMENT, NO POLLUTION CONTROLS, ETC., AND YOU'RE GOING TO HEAR A GIANT SUCKING SOUND OF JOBS BEING PULLED OUT OF THIS COUNTRY RIGHT AT A TIME WHEN WE NEED THE TAX BASE TO PAY THE DEBT."
-ROSS PEROT
"I THINK FREE TRADE IS GOING TO EXPAND OUR JOB OPPORTUNITY. I THINK IT IS EXPORTS THAT HAVE SAVED US WHEN WE'RE IN A GLOBAL SLOWDOWN, A CONNECTED GLOBAL SLOWDOWN, A RECESSION IN SOME COUNTRIES. AND IT'S FREE TRADE, FAIR TRADE, THAT NEEDS TO BE OUR HALLMARK, AND WE NEED MORE FREE TRADE AGREEMENTS, NOT FEWER."
-GEORGE H.W. BUSH

FOREIGN AID

Between $40–49 billion is expended in foreign aid yearly. That sounds like a lot to many Americans, the majority of whom are in favor of reducing it. However, a 2015 study by the Kaiser Family Foundation found that only 1 out of 20 American polled could correctly guess what percentage of the budget went to aid, with guesses averaging about 26%. The truth is that foreign aid is less than 1% of the overall budget. Not only does it provide humanitarian relief, it is also a tool that the government can use to shape political outcomes, through efforts such as peace building and reconciliation, election monitoring and support, and gender empowerment. Ever since the US instituted the **Marshall Plan** – which sought to provide economic aid to Europe in the wake of WWII as a way of creating stability that would counter the spread of communism – aid has played a large role in US strategic foreign policy. Most foreign aid is managed by the **United States Agency for International Development** (**USAID**), which is an independent governmental agency.

SOCIAL POLICYMAKING

Generally, we can say that social policymaking has two goals. The first is to create a **social safety net** – programs the aim of which is to prevent people from falling (deeper) into poverty – available to those who meet the requirements for receiving help. The second goal is to raise the general quality of life in the nation through programs aimed at improving air quality, building infrastructure (such as roads and bridges), improving schools, managing prisons, and so forth. While the allocation of resources towards improving infrastructure may not be entirely uncontroversial, it is the first goal, determining how much the government should help economically and socially vulnerable people in society, that has generated some of the most passionate debates.

In the early days of the US, federal cash relief was limited to the most vulnerable – the old, the blind and orphans – and relief for other groups was administered by private charitable organizations or by local governments. It took almost 50 years after the end of the **Revolutionary War** (1775–83) for Congress, in 1832, to pass a pension program for veterans of the war and even longer to provide financial relief for the widows of soldiers killed in battle. Still, veterans' relief was the nation's first **entitlement program**, one in which the government provides benefits to any citizen who is eligible, regardless of need, in contrast to **means-tested entitlements**, ones in which applicants must meet eligibility requirements based on need.

NEW DEAL PROGRAMS

It was under the administration of Franklin D. Roosevelt (1933–45) that the modern social safety net really took shape, as part of his "New Deal" policy package. While the earliest part of his administration was focused on programs to provide immediate economic relief to those hardest hit by the Great Depression (1929–39), over time Roosevelt designed more complicated and lasting programs to help the poor and aging, such as the **Social Security Act** (1935), which created the Social Security program, **Aid to Families with Dependent Children**, and unemployment insurance. Roosevelt's popularity surged with these reforms, although he did face resistance from the Supreme Court, which ruled in *Morehead v. New York ex rel. Tipaldo* (1936) that the government had overstepped its powers by imposing a minimum wage upon certain industries. It seemed that some members of the Court were also set on invalidating the new Social Security Act, which they saw as an overreach of power. This led to a standoff between FDR and the Court – a conflict that fizzled out without a judgment, leaving Social Security intact.

THERE ARE TOO MANY JUSTICES WHO DON'T LIKE MY PROGRAMS. HOW ABOUT I GET TO APPOINT ONE NEW JUSTICE FOR EACH ONE THAT IS OVER 70 YEARS OLD? THAT WOULD GIVE ME THE CHANCE TO PUT 6 NEW JUSTICES IN THE COURT – ONES THAT SHARE MY VIEWS.*
*FDR TRIED TO PASS SUCH LEGISLATION WITH THE JUDICIAL PROCEDURES REFORM BILL (1937), BUT IT WAS DEFEATED.

SOCIAL SECURITY

The goal of the Social Security program was to provide a minimum income for poor beneficiaries at retirement age, in which the benefits received would bear some relationship to the payroll taxes that a person had paid into it over their lifetime. For a long time, social security was fairly unproblematic, with young workers building up a "trust fund" of money for later retirees. However, as the population has aged there have been more and more elderly claiming benefits, with fewer people paying in. Social security has largely become a "pay as you go" system: workers today are financing the elderly of today. It is estimated that the "trust fund" will be exhausted by 2035, at which time the number of workers will not be able to finance the number of elderly claiming benefits.

THE WAR ON POVERTY

After the relative prosperity of the 1950's, the 60's found the nation reawakening to the reality that a significant portion of the population was still living in poverty, particularly African Americans. Lyndon B. Johnson's administration (1963–9) initiated a "War on Poverty" as part of his comprehensive "**Great Society**" program. There was a feeling that the nation was affluent enough to tackle poverty, and the hope was that a comprehensive program would raise incomes enough that fewer people would be dependent upon welfare, the costs of which had begun to rise significantly. Daniel Patrick Moynihan authored an enormously influential report on the state of black families in America, arguing that there was a breakdown in family life that was both a symptom of and a contributor to persistent poverty among blacks – an assertion that outraged many civil rights leaders.

YOU REALLY CAN'T UNDERSTAND THE WAR ON POVERTY WITHOUT UNDERSTANDING RACIAL POLITICS OF THE TIME.
THERE WAS TONS OF WHITE POVERTY IN THE 60'S, BUT FOR MANY THE FACE OF POVERTY WAS BLACK AND URBAN.
THE MOYNIHAN REPORT MADE BLACK POVERTY SEEM PATHOLOGICAL.
STILL, LOCAL BLACK ORGANIZATIONS LEVERAGED RESOURCES FROM THE COMMUNITY ACTION PROGRAM TO FURTHER CIVIL RIGHTS ACTION, SO SOME POSITIVE CHANGE DID COME OUT OF IT.

MEDICARE AND MEDICAID

Unfortunately, Johnson's programs did not significantly change the level of poverty in the United States and, in the end, the War on Poverty was widely considered a failure. However, many of the programs he created continue to this day. Notably, it was under his administration that Medicare and Medicaid were created. Medicare is a federal health insurance entitlement program aimed at helping people who are over 65 or have a severe disability (regardless of income). Medicaid is a means-tested entitlement program that provides health insurance to low-income individuals.

PERSONAL RESPONSIBILITY AND WORK OPPORTUNITY ACT

The provision of welfare has always generated controversy in the US. President Richard Nixon (1969–74) was determined to undo Johnson's Great Society, in particular welfare programs, but meaningful reform was cut short by his resignation from office. Every president after him promised some level of welfare reform, but it was under Bill Clinton (1993–2001) that the system was overhauled with the Personal Responsibility and Work Opportunity Act (1996). Aid to Families with Dependent Children was replaced with **Temporary Assistance to Needy Families (TANF)**, a program that required most recipients of aid to find work after two years of assistance. The program was bolstered by increased funding for childcare, guaranteed health insurance for recipients, and stronger efforts to enforce child support payments. Money to run the program was given to the states, and they were incentivized to get people off assistance, which led some states to make strict rules for applicants and recipients.

THE AFFORDABLE CARE ACT

Medicare and Medicaid only help a certain portion of the population in the US with healthcare costs. Until the passing of the **Affordable Care Act (ACA)** by President Obama in 2010 (also known as "**Obamacare**"), most individuals (or the businesses that employed them) had to purchase their insurance on the private marketplace; it was estimated that, on the eve of the ACA's passing, there were over 48 million uninsured people and that bankruptcies due to medical debt constituted 18–25% of all bankruptcies filed. This number of uninsured decreased to about 28 million by the end of 2016. Yet, the ACA, which fined individuals who did not obtain health insurance, was enormously unpopular with the Republican voter base, who saw it as an intrusion into their right to choose whether or not they wanted to be insured.

ENVIRONMENTAL POLICY

So far we have primarily discussed distributive and redistributive policies, but much of the work government does in terms of protecting the environment involves regulatory policy. For much of the US's history, the government did not engage in much environmental regulation, focusing instead on wilderness conservation and the creation of public parks. While some laws were passed, such as the **Migratory Bird Treaty Act** (1918), it wasn't until the environmental movement took hold in the late 1960's and early 70's that a serious regulatory agenda was set forth. Many trace the origins of the movement to the 1962 publication of the biologist Rachel Carson's book *Silent Spring*, in which she warned of the devastating effects of the use of pesticides. A groundswell of activism led to a host of legislation: the **Clean Air Act** (1970), the establishment of the **Environmental Protection Agency (EPA)** and a Council on Environmental Quality (1970), and the **Endangered Species Act** (1973) being just some examples.

WE STILL TALK IN TERMS OF CONQUEST. WE STILL HAVEN'T BECOME MATURE ENOUGH TO THINK OF OURSELVES AS ONLY A TINY PART OF A VAST AND INCREDIBLE UNIVERSE. MAN'S ATTITUDE TOWARD NATURE IS TODAY CRITICALLY IMPORTANT SIMPLY BECAUSE WE HAVE NOW ACQUIRED A FATEFUL POWER TO ALTER AND DESTROY NATURE.
RACHEL CARSON

GLOBAL WARMING

There is a global consensus among scientists that the dangers of climate change are real and pressing, but in the US adherence to international treaties aimed at reducing the human contribution to it and enacting regulation to reduce greenhouse gas emissions have been a topic of great debate, often partisan in nature. A recent poll revealed that only 30% of Republican voters (and just 17% of conservative Republicans) believe global warming is caused by human activity; instead most believe it to be due to natural changes in the environment. This is in sharp contrast to Democrats, of whom 79% believe in the human contribution to global warming. President Obama signed an executive order adopting the **Paris Climate Agreement**, a UN agreement aimed at reducing greenhouse gas emissions, but in 2017 President Trump said he would withdraw from the agreement, arguing that it was harmful to American business interests. Because of the provisions of the agreement, such a withdrawal couldn't formally happen until November 5, 2020.

THE WAR ON DRUGS

It was President Nixon who, in 1971, first declared a "War on Drugs," signing the **Controlled Substances Act** (**CSA**, 1971) into law and creating the **US Drug Enforcement Administration** (**DEA**) in 1973 to enforce drug law both domestically and internationally. Under President Ronald Reagan, it reached a new height with his and First Lady Nancy Reagan's "Just Say No" campaign - a policy that saw drug use not as a national health problem but a crime issue. Reagan enacted mandatory minimum sentencing (where judges are ordered to give a one-size-fits-all sentence) for drug crimes under the **Anti-Drug Abuse Act** (1986). It mandated the same minimum sentence of 5 years without parole for possession of 500 grams of powder cocaine as for just 5 grams of crack cocaine - a 100:1 difference. Crack (a much cheaper drug) was disproportionately used among poor people of color, who, as a result, ended up in prison more often for drug crimes.

IN 2006, AN ACLU 20-YEAR ANNIVERSARY STUDY OF THE EFFECTS OF THE ANTI-DRUG ABUSE ACT FOUND...
...THAT WHILE AFRICAN AMERICANS MADE UP 15% OF THE COUNTRY'S DRUG USERS...
...THEY COMPRISED 37% OF THOSE ARRESTED FOR DRUG VIOLATIONS...
...59% OF THOSE CONVICTED...
...AND 74% OF THOSE SENTENCED TO PRISON FOR A DRUG OFFENSE.
IN 2008 AFRICAN AMERICANS MADE UP 38% OF THE PRISON POPULATION, THOUGH THEY COMPRISE JUST 13% OF THE NATION'S POPULATION.

LEGALIZING MARIJUANA

In recent years, the War on Drugs has softened to some degree – the evolution of attitudes and policymaking around the use of marijuana being a key example. The 1970's saw a number of states decriminalizing the possession of small amounts of the drug. In 1996, California became the first state to legalize the medical use of marijuana and, since that time, other states have either decriminalized or legalized the drug for either medical or recreational use. Operating a cannabis-related business or utilizing medicinal marijuana across states is somewhat complicated, however, as the drug is still illegal at the federal level and listed by the Controlled Substances Act as a "Schedule I" drug (meaning it is seen as one with high potential for abuse, no acceptable medical use, and which would not be safe to use even under medical supervision). The DEA could take action against the marijuana industry in states in which it is legal.

THE OPIOID EPIDEMIC

While attitudes towards marijuana may have softened, there is a growing realization that drug use continues to be a significant problem in the US. In 2016, 116 people died every day from opioid-related drug overdoses (involving heroin or painkillers like oxycodone, hydrocodone, and fentanyl). Between 2000 and 2015, over half a million individuals died from overdoses. In 2017 President Trump declared the opioid epidemic a "national health emergency," which opened up agencies to devote more funds to the issue. The Drug Enforcement Administration (DEA), a law enforcement agency under the Department of Justice, is charged with enforcing laws concerning controlled substances.

PRISONS AND THE CRIMINAL JUSTICE SYSTEM

One often-quoted statistic is that while the US has around 5% of the world's population, it has almost 25% of the world's prisoners. While the exact numbers might be debatable (getting accurate numbers for China, for example, is very difficult), few dispute the fact that the US leads the world in incarcerations. The prison system is a massive: it has an estimated operating cost of $80 billion a year; people are sent to jail close to 11 million times each year; and 1.5 million individuals are held at any one time in state and federal prisons (up from 320,000 in 1980). Around 5 million Americans are on parole or supervision.

An administration's policymaking choices can have a direct effect on the number of incarcerated individuals, as decisions at the federal level to increase enforcement of certain crimes shapes local law enforcement priorities.

IT IS SO TRUE THAT THE PEOPLE IN CHARGE AT THE LOCAL LEVEL CAN REALLY AFFECT WHO GOES TO JAIL.
THE DISTRICT ATTORNEY, WHO'S IN CHARGE OF ALL THE STATE PROSECUTORS, HAS A LOT OF POWER. THEY DECIDE WHAT TYPE OF CRIMES ARE GOING TO BE AGGRESSIVELY PURSUED.
THEY'RE ELECTED, BUT IT ISN'T A JOB THAT MOST VOTERS REALLY UNDERSTAND.

MILITARY PRISONS

In addition to state and federal prisons, the US also runs military prisons, located across the world. They are used to hold members of the military found guilty of serious crimes, as well as prisoners of war and "enemy combatants." While prisoners of war are subject to certain protections under the **Geneva Convention** – a set of international treaties and protocols for humanitarian treatment in warfare – enemy combatants (who are seen as rogue elements acting outside of the laws and customs of warfare) are not.

Two military prisons, the **Guantanamo Bay detention camp** and the **Abu Ghraib prison** in Iraq (now closed), came under controversy for alleged human rights abuses. Guantanamo Bay was established after the terrorist attacks of 9/11 as part of George W. Bush's **War on Terror**. The Bush administration argued that the detainees were enemy combatants and not due the rights of prisoners of war, but the Supreme Court ruled in *Hamdan v. Rumsfeld* (2006) that they were entitled to some minimal protections under Article 3 of the Geneva Convention.

I REMEMBER WHEN OBAMA SAID HE WAS GOING TO CLOSE GUANTANAMO.
IN THE DARK HALLS OF ABU GHRAIB AND THE DETENTION CELLS OF GUANTANAMO, WE HAVE COMPROMISED OUR MOST PRECIOUS VALUES.
HE EVEN ISSUED AN EXECUTIVE ORDER THAT IT BE CLOSED WITHIN A YEAR.
HAVE YOU HEARD? WE'RE GETTING OUT OF HERE!
BUT IT DIDN'T WORK OUT. I THINK LIKE 40 PEOPLE ARE STILL THERE. SO DISAPPOINTING.

IMMIGRATION

Immigration has played a large role in the growth and development of the United States, but throughout its history attitudes towards immigration, or certain types of immigrants, have varied widely. In 1882, for example, the **Chinese Exclusion Act** passed, which prohibited the immigration of Chinese laborers. It wasn't repealed until 1943. The **Immigration and Naturalization Act** (1952) became the governing body of law concerning immigration. From the 1920's until 1965, immigration was governed by a system of quotas, in which immigrants and refugees from certain countries (typically Northern and Western Europeans) were given preference over others (such as those from African nations). This was changed in 1965 by the **Immigration and Nationality Act (INA)**. While quotas weren't abolished, the emphasis was changed from nationality to granting visas to the family of current US residents – in other words, for family reunification.

MEXICAN IMMIGRATION

The 1960's also brought a huge change in the status of immigration from Mexico. To address the lack of agricultural workers during WWII, the **Emergency Farm Labor Supply Program Agreement** (1942) was put into law between the US and Mexico, aka the Bracero Program. This law allowed Mexican nationals to work in the US temporarily via labor contracts. Overall, 4.6 million contracts were signed. The program ended in 1964, and just a year later the Immigration and Nationality Act, for the first time, created limits on Mexican immigration. The next major piece of legislation came under the Reagan Administration in 1986: the **Immigration Reform and Control Act (IRCA)**. It gave legal status to qualified undocumented immigrants who had entered the country before 1982 but also created stricter laws regarding border control and the hiring of undocumented Mexican workers. Today, Mexican immigrants make up about 28% of foreign-born residents in the US.

DEFERRED ACTION FOR CHILDHOOD ARRIVALS

Many undocumented immigrants in the US were brought in as children. In 2012, through an executive order, President Obama signed **Deferred Action for Childhood Arrivals (DACA)** into law, which provided relief for such individuals. DACA is not a path to citizenship. Rather, it gives successful applicants a renewable 2-year deferrance from deportation and the ability to apply for a work permit. In order to qualify, applicants must: have been brought to the US before the age of 16 (and before June 2007); be under 31 years old; have lived continuously in the US; have completed high school or GED, served honorably in the military or currently attend school; and have a criminal record with no felonies or serious misdemeanors. The nearly 800,000 participants are known as "Dreamers," a name which came from an earlier **Development, Relief, and Education for Alien Minors Act (DREAM)** bill, which had been introduced unsuccessfully several times in Congress since 2001. Unlike DACA, the DREAM bill included a path to citizenship.

Attitudes towards immigration, like many issues in the US, tend to be partisan. The Republican party takes a tough stance on what they refer to as "illegal" immigration, arguing that any immigration policy must "put the interests of existing citizens first." Donald Trump's campaign garnered strong support among his political base for the idea of building a wall between the US and Mexico and creating travel bans and "extreme vetting" for immigrants from predominantly Muslim nations. Democrats tend to be more sympathetic towards immigration, seeing it not just a problem that needs to be solved but, according to their party platform, as "a defining aspect of the American character and our shared history."

GIVE ME YOUR TIRED, YOUR POOR, YOUR HUDDLED MASSES YEARNING TO BREATHE FREE, THE WRETCHED REFUSE OF YOUR TEEMING SHORE. SEND THESE, THE HOMELESS, TEMPEST-TOST TO ME, I LIFT MY LAMP BESIDE THE GOLDEN DOOR!

A COMPETITIVE IMMIGRATION APPLICATION PROCESS WILL FAVOR APPLICANTS WHO CAN SPEAK ENGLISH, FINANCIALLY SUPPORT THEMSELVES AND THEIR FAMILIES AND DEMONSTRATE SKILLS THAT WILL CONTRIBUTE TO OUR ECONOMY. THEY'RE NOT GOING TO COME IN AND IMMEDIATELY GO AND COLLECT WELFARE.

GUN CONTROL

In 2012, a man fatally shot 20 children between the ages of 6 and 7, as well as 6 staff members, his mother, and then himself. The Sandy Hook Elementary massacre, as much as it shocked the nation, did not result in significant changes in gun legislation. Gun rights advocates argue that these types of shootings are primarily a mental health issue, which cannot be solved by reducing the number or type of guns available. Still, in the 5 years after Sandy Hook, there were 1,600 mass shootings in the US. (Mass shootings are defined as 4 or more people shot at the same general time and location.) The partial restrictions on gun ownership passed after subsequent mass shootings are generally seen by gun control advocates as a far from satisfying response.

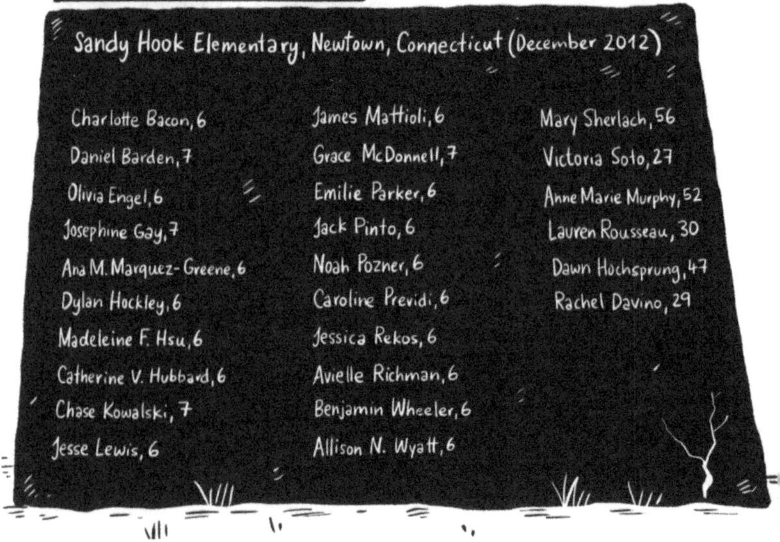

Those in favor of gun restrictions point to the fact that, with 27 Americans shot dead every day, the United States is an extreme outlier in the world. Internationally, only Guatemala, Mexico, and the US have a constitutionally enshrined right of citizens to bear arms. However, the culture of gun ownership in the US is strong. Currently, about 42% of Americans say that they have a gun in their home, which (if correct) means around 80 million gun owners. Restrictions have been extremely difficult to pass, in part because of the strength of the National Rifle Association (NRA), an interest group established in 1871 that is devoted to protecting the ability of Americans to buy and trade guns with as few restrictions as possible. The NRA claims over 5 million members and, as we saw earlier in the book, it spent almost $55 million during the 2016 federal election cycle to elect pro-gun politicians.

FEDERAL GUN RESTRICTIONS

There are restrictions and laws regarding gun sales and ownership. The **National Firearms Act** (1934) imposed a $200 tax on certain firearms (short-barrel shotguns, silencers, and machine guns) in an effort to curtail their use. After President John F. Kennedy was assassinated with a gun purchased through the mail, Congress passed the **Gun Control Act** (1968), which prohibited the mail order purchase of guns. It also banned certain categories of people from owning a gun (felons, drug users, and the mentally incompetent), although state laws can reinstate the ability of someone in these categories to own a gun, as in Texas, where a felon can keep one in their residence 5 years after their felony was discharged. The Gun Control Act was bolstered by the **Brady Handgun Violence Prevention Act** (1993), which (among other provisions) required that individuals wishing to purchase a gun pass a background check and wait a mandatory 5-day period before completing their purchase. The mandatory waiting period was eliminated when the FBI's **National Instant Criminal Background Check System** (**NICS**) was created.

I'M GLAD WE HAVE BACKGROUND CHECKS, BUT TOO MANY TIMES PEOPLE FALL THROUGH THE CRACKS.
YOU CAN'T SELL A GUN TO SOMEONE WHO HAS BEEN INVOLUNTARILY COMMITTED TO A MENTAL HOSPITAL, BUT OTHERWISE SELLERS CAN'T PREVENT PEOPLE FROM BUYING GUNS BASED ON MENTAL ILLNESS, EVEN THOSE WHOSE ILLNESSES MAY MAKE THEM AGGRESSIVE AND IMPULSIVE.
The
GUN SHOP
PISTOLS
RIFLES

STATE GUN RESTRICTIONS

States are allowed to pass laws that modify or complement federal laws (as we saw with laws about the consumption of marijuana). For example, federal law does not require background checks when guns are purchased from private individuals at gun shows (only licensed dealers must conduct a check). However, 6 states (California, Colorado, Illinois, New York, Oregon, and Rhode Island) require them for all sales, both public and private. Some states allow an individual to carry a concealed weapon or for the "open carry" (that is, in plain sight) of a firearm. These varied restrictions reflect each state's unique history and values in regard to gun ownership. The gun magazine *Guns and Ammo* rates Arizona the highest in terms of an individual's freedom to purchase and carry different types of guns: in that state anyone over the age of 21 who is not prohibited from owning a gun by federal law can carry one (open or concealed) without a license.

YOU USED TO BE ALLOWED TO OPENLY CARRY A LOADED GUN IN CALIFORNIA.
THAT CHANGED WHEN, IN THE LATE 1960'S, THE BLACK PANTHERS SENT OUT ARMED MEMBERS TO SURVEIL OAKLAND POLICE OFFICERS.
BLACK PANTHER PARTY
IN 1967 THE BLACK PANTHERS WENT TO CALIFORNIA'S CAPITOL BUILDING TO PROTEST THE PASSAGE OF THE MULFORD ACT, WHICH SOUGHT TO MAKE THE OPEN CARRY OF LOADED GUNS ILLEGAL IN THE STATE.
THEIR PROTEST ALARMED POLITICIANS. THEY QUICKLY MOVED TO PASS THE LEGISLATION, WHICH STILL STANDS.

ECONOMIC POLICYMAKING

While social policymaking often takes center stage in the daily political arena, economic policymaking is equally important when it comes to creating a healthy nation and engaging voters. As Bill Clinton's presidential campaign made famous, when voters look to what is important to them, very often, "it's the economy, stupid." Economic policymaking can be generally divided into two categories: **fiscal** and **monetary** policy. Fiscal policy refers to spending and taxation, and monetary policy to the control of the supply of money in the economy. Fiscal policy tends to be partisan, with the Republican party's rhetoric favoring a decrease in taxation and spending, and Democrats favoring an increase in corporate and high-income taxation and an increase in spending for social welfare programs.

MONETARY POLICY: THE CENTRAL BANK

We often hear on the news that the stock market rises and falls in anticipation of, or as a reaction to, the latest announcement from **Federal Reserve System** (often referred to simply as "the Fed"). Indeed, in 1996, minutes after former Fed Chairman Alan Greenspan made a statement that he thought a recent rise in stock market value was due to "irrational exuberance," worldwide stock markets started to tumble in value, creating a domino effect that eventually led to a 4% drop in the **Dow Jones Industrial Average** (aka "the Dow"), an index of US stock values.

The actions or potential actions of the Federal Reserve System are so significant because it is the nation's central bank, established in 1913. Among other duties, it is responsible for running 12 Federal Reserve Banks and 24 branches. The Fed is supposed to be politically neutral, led by a board of governors who serve 14-year terms, and a chairman and vice-chairman who serve 4-year terms. The entire board is nominated by the president and confirmed by the Senate, and their terms are staggered so that no one president can nominate an entire board.

Former Fed Chair
ALAN GREENSPAN
SINCE BECOMING A CENTRAL BANKER, I HAVE LEARNED TO MUMBLE WITH GREAT INCOHERENCE. IF I SEEM UNDULY CLEAR TO YOU, YOU MUST HAVE MISUNDERSTOOD WHAT I SAID.

The **Federal Open Market Committee (FOMC)** is the Fed's policymaking body in charge of controlling the supply of money (all of the cash on hand and money held in checking accounts) in the economy. Since the Federal Reserve Banks are those from which other banks and institutions borrow money, the FOMC can control the money supply by raising and lowering the interest rates at which money can be borrowed, reducing the amount that banks have to keep on reserve compared to what they loan out; they can also control the supply by buying government securities. Lower interest rates encourage borrowing and spending since money is "cheaper," while higher rates encourage saving. By reducing the reserves that banks must keep, it gives them more money to lend. Changing the supply of money is a tool for controlling inflation and unemployment; when the economy is "heating up" and inflation is starting to rise, restricting the supply of money can be a way of countering that trend, although too much of a restriction can lead to a recession.

FISCAL POLICY

Economists have a number of tools for measuring the strength of the economy, but one of the most common measures is the nation's **gross domestic product (GDP)**, which gives a market value for all of the goods and services produced in a nation. Growth in GDP is rarely a smooth linear path. Rather, every economic system tends to run what is known as a business cycle: periods of economic booms (where the GDP is growing quickly) and economic busts (where there is a significant decline in the GDP). As described earlier, it was the Keynesian revolution during the Great Depression which really popularized the idea that government could (and should) smooth out the severity of the boom-bust cycle through engaging in aggressive fiscal policymaking, such as increasing or reducing government spending, taxation, or regulation.

TAXATION

Throughout the history of governance, there are few issues that have caused as much dissatisfaction and revolt as taxation. Indeed, "no taxation without representation" was the rallying cry for the American Revolution against the British. According to Article 1, Section 7 of the Constitution, the House of Representatives has the "power of the purse," as all taxation bills originate there; although bills must pass the Senate as well and be signed into law by the president. In 2016, almost $3.3 trillion was collected in taxes, the majority of which came from individual income taxes, which are derived from a **progressive** tax system, meaning those with higher incomes pay higher tax rates. Other types of taxes are **regressive**, meaning that the poor pay a proportionally larger share of their income towards the tax. For example, a sales tax is regressive, since a 5% tax on $100 worth of goods will hit a poor person harder than a rich one.

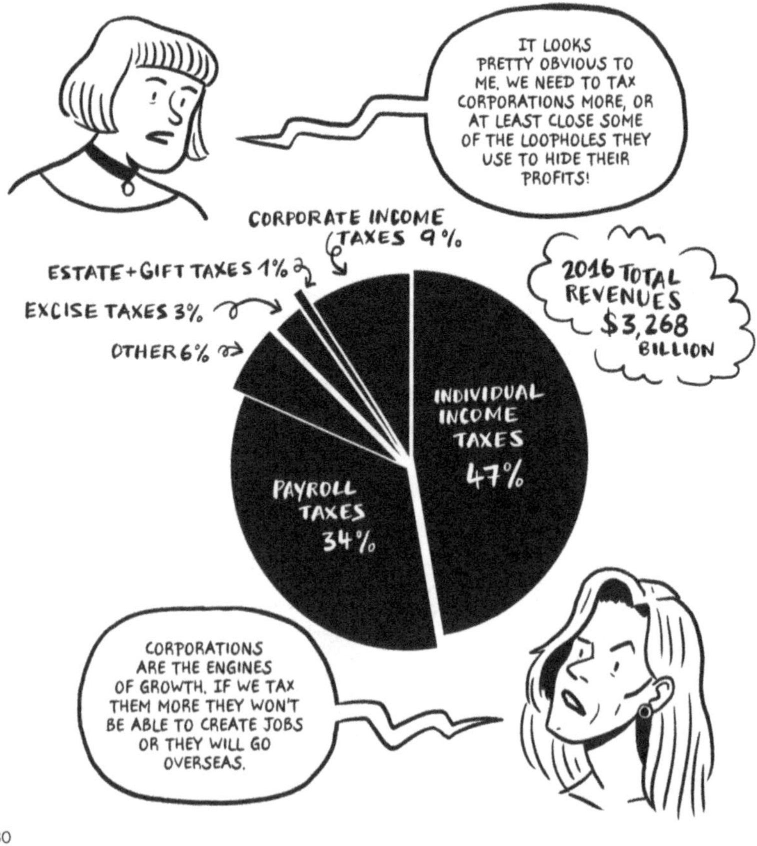

GOVERNMENT SPENDING

Government spending reflects the values and political struggles of the nation not only in the present but also in the past, through acts of prior Congresses. The budget comprises three types of spending: mandatory, discretionary, and interest on debt. **Mandatory spending** is spending on programs that were enacted through **authorization laws** (laws that authorize spending from the federal budget) in the past and for which the federal government is obligated to pay. Medicare, Social Security, and Medicaid are the largest programs, but others such as veterans' benefits and food assistance programs are also included. The government must also pay the **interest** on its debt, which is currently about 6-7% of the total budget. **Discretionary spending** encompasses everything from education to the military, transportation, and food and agriculture.

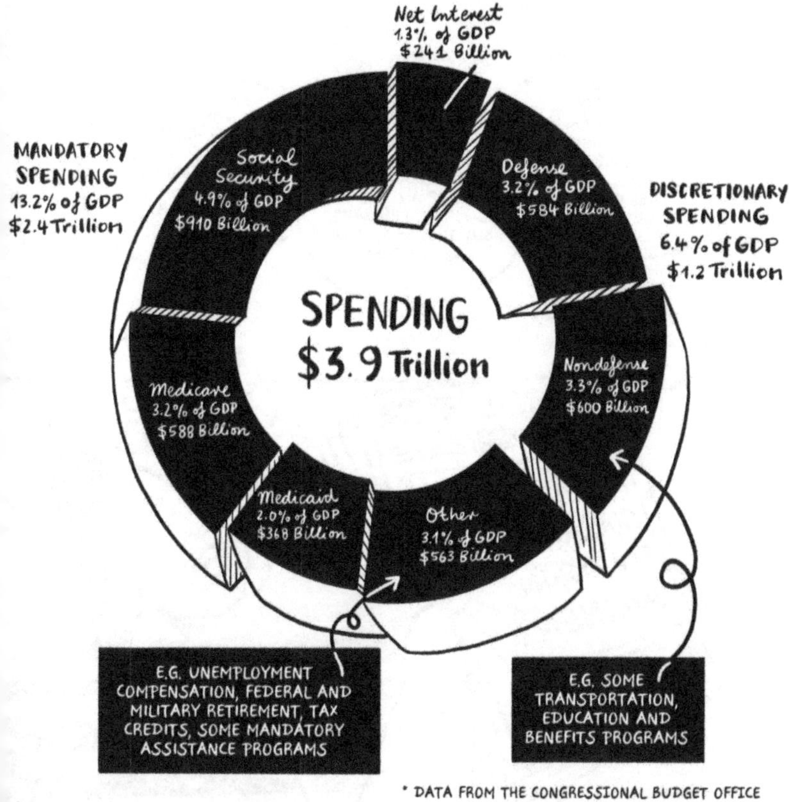

* DATA FROM THE CONGRESSIONAL BUDGET OFFICE

NATIONAL DEBT

It is not uncommon for politicians on the campaign trail to make promises that, if actually enacted, could be costly. Once in office, it can be difficult to uphold those promises, since increased spending can only come from higher taxes or increased borrowing. Since taxes are unpopular, it can be tempting to borrow the money needed to achieve policy goals. Where does that money come from? The US government doesn't go to foreign banks and apply for a loan. Rather, it "issues" debt by selling US Treasury securities – bills, notes, bonds, Treasury Inflation-Protected Securities (TIPS), and savings bonds – to individuals, businesses, state and local governments in the US, and abroad. The **national debt** reached over $20 trillion in 2018, which equates to about $171,000 per taxpayer. The government isn't allowed to borrow an infinite amount of money; there is a **debt ceiling** above which it cannot rise, unless Congress votes to raise the ceiling, which it did 14 times between 2001–16.

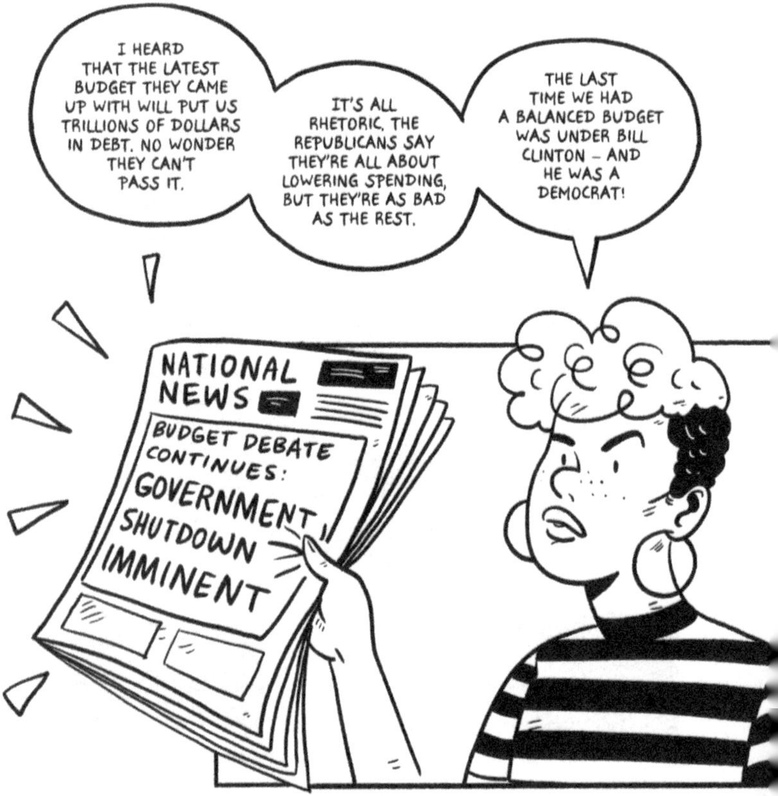

REGULATORY POLICYMAKING

Taxation and spending tend to be a type of **redistributive policymaking** (in which wealth is shifted from one group to another, such as with food stamps) or **distributive policymaking** (where money is taken from the whole to address the needs of smaller groups, such as providing tax deductions for homeowners). A third form of policymaking is **regulatory**, which aims to control the actions of individuals or groups, for the benefit of the whole. Economic regulatory policymaking tends to involve the regulation of business, labor, and trade. Both proposed and final regulations must be made public in the Federal Register, a daily publication that is the official journal of the US federal government.

REGULATORY POLICYMAKING IN BUSINESS

The government regulates many aspects of business operations: the **Food and Drug Administration (FDA)** regulates what goes into food and medicine; the Environmental Protection Agency (EPA) sets limits on the pollution that manufacturers can emit; the **Employment Standards Administration (ESA)** enforces fair labor practices, and so forth. In addition to regulating internal practices, the government also regulates the relationships between businesses. There is a general consensus that it is unhealthy for society if one business grows so large that it dominates a market and eliminates competition, becoming a monopoly. For that reason, the government has created **antitrust policies**, which protect consumers from the formation of predatory monopolies. The most famous was the **Sherman Antitrust Act** (1890), which outlawed concerted efforts to restrain the free flow of trade by engaging in practices such as price fixing or constraining production to artificially raise prices, and which prohibited attempts to monopolize trade. In 1914 the **Federal Trade Commission (FTC)** was created to investigate potential antitrust violations, working with the **Department of Justice's Antitrust Division** after it was established in 1933.

REGULATORY POLICYMAKING: LABOR

While there were movements to improve labor conditions during the Industrial Revolution in the 19th century, it wasn't until President Roosevelt passed the **Fair Labor Standards** Act in 1938 that legislation provided comprehensive protections for all workers in the US. It created a minimum wage, a 40-hour work week with overtime pay, minimum age requirements for workers, and recordkeeping standards. The next big change came with the passing of the **National Labor Relations Act** (1935) – more commonly known as the Wagner Act – which legalized the right of workers to form unions and engage in collective bargaining. The power of unions was curtailed by the subsequent passing of the **Labor Management Relations Act** (1947), also known as the Taft-Hartley Act. Among other changes, it limited the types of strikes unions could hold (prohibiting, for example, solidarity strikes), restricted the ability of labor groups to contribute to political campaigns, and ended the ability of unions to create "closed shops": job sites in which all employees were required to join the union.

PART III: THE FOURTH BRANCH OF GOVERNMENT - THE PEOPLE

So far we have considered the relationship of Americans to their political system in terms of how they develop political ideologies and party affiliations, and we've also examined how formal institutions in society – the Constitution, the Presidency, Congress, and the Judiciary – have interacted with each other and with those people living within the United States. This part of the book will examine political action from the ground up: the media, interest groups, social movements, and campaign financing.

THE MEDIA: EARLY HISTORY

Today the term "media" encompasses a dizzying number of ways of communicating information: books, magazines, newspapers, radio, podcasts, television, movies, music, electronic media, billboards, and so on. Before the invention of the television and radio, the newspaper was the most influential form of mass media in the United States – considered so critical that the **US Postal Service Act** (1792) allowed the cost of mailing newspapers to the public to be subsidized. The development of high-speed printing presses in the 1830's gave rise to the **penny press**: daily penny newspapers that tended towards sensationalism rather than hard journalism. Still, across the nation, rural and small-town newspapers served to help keep isolated members of society abreast of political developments, if at a delay. The problem of communicating news events in a timely manner changed in the 1940's with the invention of the telegraph – which allowed news to be transmitted instantaneously over long distances, along a wire – and the formation of an **Associated Press**, which shared news at first in the New York region, then nationally and internationally.

Radio was the next big development in the spread of mass communication, starting in the 1920's but reaching its height as a key source of entertainment and information in the late 40's and early 50's, until the television gained popularity. Early radio could be a political tool. President Franklin D. Roosevelt used the radio to communicate with voters through a series of broadcasts from 1933–44, which became known as his "**fireside chats**." While not actually recorded at a fireside, the term evoked the intimate, relatable, and calming influence Roosevelt sought to achieve during the tumultuous events of the Great Depression and World War II. Regulation of radio broadcasting has its origins in the **Radio Act** (1927), which created a regulatory governmental agency for the medium, eventually named the **Federal Communications Commission** (**FCC**), which remains in existence today. It also regulates the television industry.

THE MEDIA: RELATIONSHIP TO THE WHITE HOUSE

While there is no law that enshrines the press's ability to directly access the White House, for as long as both have been in existence, the press has gone to the White House for information to report. The White House Correspondents' Association (WHCA) was formed in 1914, in response to a rumor (unfounded) that Congress planned to restrict attendance to President Woodrow Wilson's press conferences. The Association still exists (although not every reporter with access is a member), notably hosting the White House Correspondents' Dinner, a fun event at which the press and the president trade friendly jabs. Not every reporter can become part of the White House press pool. They must first be approved for a press pass by the **Standing Committee of Correspondents**, a congressional committee created in 1879, which is made up of reporters, after which they must receive security clearance.

"I KNOW THAT THERE ARE TIMES THAT WE'VE HAD DIFFERENCES, AND THAT'S INHERENT IN OUR INSTITUTIONAL ROLES – IT'S TRUE OF EVERY PRESIDENT AND HIS PRESS CORPS. BUT WE'VE ALWAYS SHARED THE SAME GOAL – TO ROOT OUR PUBLIC DISCOURSE IN THE TRUTH; TO OPEN THE DOORS OF THIS DEMOCRACY; TO DO WHATEVER WE CAN TO MAKE OUR COUNTRY AND OUR WORLD MORE FREE AND MORE JUST."
THE PRESIDENT OF THE UNITED

Every president has had a different relationship to the press. It was Theodore Roosevelt (1901–9) who really initiated an active courting of the press, giving them their own office in the West Wing and often briefing them during his morning shave. John F. Kennedy (1961–3) was the first president to air live press briefings without editing or delay – holding an average of two per month – with an audience so large that they eventually had to hold them in an auditorium that could seat 800 people. Sometimes the president chooses to directly engage reporters, but often information is conveyed through the White House Press Secretary, who holds periodic press conferences. During times of scandal or stress, the relationship can become contentious, particularly with certain news outlets, if the president doesn't like what is being reported or how.

THE MEDIA: SATIRE

Satire has been an important form of political engagement since the dawn of politics. In Greece, the playwright Aristophanes (b. 450 BC) used the comedic form to critique the politics of his day. In the United States, the use of satire has a long history, from newspaper comics to literature, theater, music, television, and media sites. Television shows such as *The Daily Show* or *The Colbert Report* (and, more recently, newer shows like *Full Frontal with Samantha Bee* or *Last Week Tonight with John Oliver)* provided almost daily satiric commentary on the political events of the day, as well as critiquing the media itself. Among millennials, particularly liberal ones, these shows became a trusted news source, with a 2015 Public Religion Research Institute poll finding that 10% of Americans between the ages of 18–29 trusted *The Daily Show* or *The Colbert Report* "the most to tell them what's going on in the world."

THE MEDIA: SOCIAL MEDIA

With billions of users, social media platforms like Facebook, Twitter, Instagram, Reddit, and Tumbler (or the many hundreds of specialized sites), allow users both to make personal connections and to try to understand the world around them. However, what is increasingly understood is that social media often *doesn't* expose users to diverse viewpoints, instead putting people into a "filter bubble," where they tend to see information that confirms their own interests and viewpoints. *The Wall Street Journal* created a tool it calls Blue Feed, Red Feed, where users can see the same issue as it appears from each side of the ideological spectrum on Facebook. It shows how the exact same issue or event can be presented in very different ways, encouraging **confirmation bias**, the tendency to interpret new information in such a way that confirms our existing beliefs.

THE MEDIA: THE 24-HOUR NEWS CYCLE

While 10% of Americans may call satirical shows like *The Daily Show* their most trusted news source, the majority of Americans (54%) trust the Cable News Network (CNN) the most. CNN was really the founder of what is known as the 24-hour news cycle; it launched in 1980 to provide round-the-clock news coverage. With the growing availability of cable TV to American households in the 1990's, the number of news networks began to expand, with MSNBC and Fox News both launching in 1996. Critics argue that the drive to be the first network to provide "breaking" coverage has led to a weakening of serious, investigative journalism; that the repetition of stories can create a desensitization of the public to important issues; and that featured talk news shows act more as ideological echo chambers than as serious platforms for substantive debate. On the other hand, the massive resources of the major news channels allows them to put reporters "on the ground" in many countries, allowing for a first-hand view of major news developments worldwide.

THE MEDIA: FAKE NEWS?

While President Donald Trump wasn't the first to use the term "fake news," he made the phrase his own, constantly claiming that certain news outlets were making false or misleading reports. The phrase has become a rallying cry in an era when, in fact, people do have a hard time discerning what information to trust, particularly in news received via social media. And yet, it is important to differentiate between news that is deliberately misleading and news that one simply doesn't like; too often it is easy for someone to cry "fake news" when the information it contains is damaging to themselves or their party.

HOW TO SPOT FAKE NEWS
CONSIDER THE SOURCE
CLICK AWAY FROM THE STORY TO INVESTIGATE THE SITE, ITS MISSION AND ITS CONTACT INFO.
READ BEYOND
HEADLINES CAN BE OUTRAGEOUS IN AN EFFORT TO GET CLICKS. WHAT'S THE WHOLE STORY?
CHECK THE AUTHOR
DO A QUICK SEARCH ON THE AUTHOR. ARE THEY CREDIBLE? ARE THEY REAL?
SUPPORTING SOURCES?
CLICK ON THOSE LINKS. DETERMINE IF THE INFO GIVEN ACTUALLY SUPPORTS THE STORY.
CHECK THE DATE
REPOSTING OLD NEWS STORIES DOESN'T MEAN THEY'RE RELEVANT TO CURRENT EVENTS.
IS IT A JOKE?
IF IT IS TOO OUTLANDISH, IT MIGHT BE SATIRE. RESEARCH THE SITE AND AUTHOR TO BE SURE.
CHECK YOUR BIASES
CONSIDER IF YOUR OWN BELIEFS COULD AFFECT YOUR JUDGEMENT.
HOO!
ASK THE EXPERTS
ASK A LIBRARIAN, OR CONSULT A FACT-CHECKING SITE.
BASED ON THE IFLA'S GRAPHIC "HOW TO SPOT FAKE NEWS", FROM STEPS CREATED BY FACTCHECK.ORG

INTEREST GROUPS: THE DANGERS OF FACTION

Just as with the media, Americans also tend to have a love/hate relationship with populist interest groups, viewing the information they provide to the public and to politicians as biased and serving the interests of the few, rather than the many. That love/hate feeling goes all the way back to the founding of the nation. James Madison, in his Federalist Paper #10, warned of what he considered the "mischiefs of faction." By "faction" he meant a group of people who were united by a passion or cause, one which could be considered adverse to the rights of others or to the community as a whole. Madison felt that factions were impossible to get rid of, as they are borne of the liberty that is an essential component of democracy. His feeling seems to be generally shared today. Although people may be concerned about the "special interests" that shape politics (particularly wealthy interests), reform has been slow in coming.

IT JUST SEEMS LIKE PEOPLE HATE INTEREST GROUPS WHEN IT IS SOMETHING THEY DON'T AGREE WITH. IF GREENPEACE HAD AS MUCH MONEY AS THE NRA, WOULD YOU STILL BE COMPLAINING?
THAT'S NOT TRUE. WE JUST DON'T THINK THAT PUBLIC POLICY SHOULD BE DRIVEN BY WHICH GROUPS HAVE THE MOST MONEY TO SPEND ON POLITICS.

THE PROFESSIONALIZATION OF GROUPS

How interest groups have formed and functioned has shifted over the last century. Political scientist **Theda Skocpol** (b. 1947) argues that in the 1940's and 50's, issue advocacy primarily came out of broad-based membership associations, but that in more recent years there has been a professionalization of interest groups: people pay their membership dues and the professionals do the lobbying. Such groups utilize a number of incentives to gain members: providing discounts, insurance, and, of course, and, of course, a way to support a cause (potential) members believe in. The enormously influential **American Association of Retired Persons** (**AARP**), with a membership base of over 37 million, is an example of one such group. The problem, Skocpol argues, is that when decisions about advocacy are made by elite lobbying professionals, it turns group members into "detached spectators" and detracts from the democratic nature of interest groups.

CAMPAIGN FINANCE

Concurrent with the rise in professionalism in interest group advocacy is a rise in the amount of money those interest groups donate and spend on elections in the United States. Such election financing is categorized as "hard" or "soft" money. **Hard money** is donated to campaigns and is regulated by the Federal Election Commission and subject to limits. **Soft money** is used towards ambiguously defined "party building" activities and is not regulated. Money can be donated or spent by individual interest groups, like the AARP, or groups can combine resources. A **political action committee** (**PAC**) collects money from multiple groups' members to influence elections. It cannot accept money from unions or corporations. A **super PAC**, also known as an "independent-expenditure only committee," can spend unlimited amounts of money on political parties, as long as that money is not directed towards particular campaigns.

ADVOCACY GROUPS and their REGULATIONS	CONTRIBUTION LIMIT	MUST DISCLOSE DONORS?	CAN CO-ORDINATE WITH CANDIDATE	CAN BE PRIMARILY POLITICAL?	CAN EXPRESSLY TELL VOTERS WHO TO VOTE FOR?	REGULATOR
Traditional PACs	$5,000 per year	YES	YES	YES	YES	FEC
Super PAC	Unlimited	YES	NO	YES	YES	FEC
501 (c)(4) NON-PROFIT	Unlimited	NO	NO	NO	NO	IRS
527 NON-PROFIT	Unlimited	YES	NO	YES	NO	FEC

CAMPAIGN FINANCE: REFORM EFFORTS

Reforming campaign finance laws really began in earnest with the **Federal Election Campaign Act** (1971), which required the disclosure of money spent on politics over $200. Limits on expenditures didn't exist until the act was amended in 1974, creating at the same time the **Federal Election Commission** (**FEC**), whose job it was to enforce federal campaign finance laws. Among other provisions, the 1974 act limited individual donations to $1,000 and donations by PACs to $5,000. This act was amended several times after the Supreme Court decision in *Buckley v. Valeo* (1976) decided that a number of the provisions in the act were a violation of free speech – such as the limitation on the amount of money a candidate or party could spend on an election, and the limitation on **independent expenditures** (money spent in an election by individuals or groups other than candidates or parties that are not made on behalf of or by request of those candidates or parties).

CAMPAIGN FINANCE: THE BCRA AND CITIZENS UNITED

In 2008, the nonprofit Citizens United produced ***Hillary: The Movie***, a film which argued that Hillary Clinton, then a presidential candidate, was unfit for the office. Citizens United wanted to air the movie right before the Democratic Primary, which the FEC decided would be at odds with the **Bipartisan Campaign Reform Act** (**BCRA**, 2002). In addition to placing stronger restrictions on the use of soft money in elections, the BCRA created strict rules around "electioneering communications" – any communication regarding a particular candidate made 60 days before a general election or 30 days before a primary – and, notably, it prohibited corporations and unions from funding them. In the Supreme Court case ***Citizens United v. Federal Election Commission*** (2010), Citizens United successfully argued that the film was not electioneering and thus not subject to FEC regulation. The Court also decided that the BCRA's restriction of corporate spending was an unconstitutional restriction on free speech.

IT IS TOTALLY HYPOCRITICAL THAT THE SAME LIBERALS WHO GO ON AND ON ABOUT FREE SPEECH GOT IN SUCH A TIZZY ABOUT CITIZENS UNITED.
FREEDOM TO SPEND MONEY AND FREEDOM OF SPEECH ARE NOT THE SAME THING!
COME ON. WITHOUT MONEY, IDEAS GET NO EXPOSURE. YOU CAN STAND ON A STREET CORNER YELLING YOUR THOUGHTS, AND THAT MAY REACH A FEW PEOPLE, BUT IF YOU HAVE THE MONEY TO BUY A BULLHORN, YOU'LL BE A LOT MORE EFFECTIVE.
BUT IF ONLY CORPORATE EXECUTIVES CAN AFFORD A BULLHORN, IS THAT FAIR? HOW WILL THE VOICES OF ORDINARY PEOPLE BE HEARD?

A NATION OF JOINERS

In 2000, the political scientist Robert Putnam published a book entitled ***Bowling Alone***, in which he argued that Americans were no longer meeting up face-to-face and making meaningful connections like they did in the 1950's and 60's. For example, instead of bowling in leagues, they were now (as the title suggests) bowling alone. While the levels to which Americans belong to local groups based on shared interests may rise and fall over time, overall they have a long history of joining and belonging. One of the earliest studies of this tendency was Alexis de Tocqueville's study of American society, *Democracy in America*, published in 1835. De Tocqueville observed that Americans tend to form deliberative groups or associations at a local level and to be active political participants in the democratic system. He argued that associational activity in America was what made the American democratic experiment possible and countered tendencies towards tyranny.

SOCIAL MOVEMENTS

Lasting change often comes through social movements – membership of which often comes about through activation after a significant event, recruitment, or shifts in the political landscape. It is impossible to discuss all of the most significant social movements here, but we will highlight a few historical ones and then move on to consider some of the more contemporary movements.

THE ABOLITIONIST MOVEMENT

The abolitionist movement aimed to end slavery, racial segregation, and discrimination. One of the earliest and most militant abolitionists was a free black man named **David Walker**. In 1829, he published a pamphlet entitled "An Appeal to the Coloured Citizens of the World," which justified using violence in the fight for freedom, arguing that: "it is no more harm for you to kill a man who is trying to kill you, than it is for you to take a drink of water when thirsty." An influential white ally, William Lloyd Garrison, started the abolitionist paper *The Liberator* in 1830 and helped found the **New England Anti-Slavery Society**. After Walker's death, he published excerpts of his work in *The Liberator*.

The abolitionist movement grew, up to the start of the Civil War between the North and South in 1861, which lasted 4 years. In 1863, as a war tactic, President Abraham Lincoln signed an executive order known as the **Emancipation Proclamation**, which freed Southern slaves. Accordingly, slaves who could escape were considered free once they reached Northern soil, and many newly freed blacks joined the war against the South. It did not, however, free *all* slaves nor grant citizenship to former slaves. Slavery wasn't abolished until the ratification of the 13th Amendment in 1865. **Frederick Douglass** (1818–95), a former slave who was one of the abolitionist movement's most powerful activists and orators, met personally with President Lincoln in 1863 to discuss how to make the war effort more inclusive for black soldiers.

WOMEN'S RIGHTS: VOTING

The birth of the women's rights movement is generally dated to 1848, to Seneca Falls, New York, where a group of women called "a convention to discuss the social, civil, and religious condition and rights of woman." The "Declaration of Sentiments, Grievances, and Resolutions" drafted at the convention contained 12 resolutions that were passed unanimously and one that was not - calling for the right to vote. The question of women's **suffrage** was almost as divisive for the movement as it was for the nation in general, and it took 72 more years for women to be granted the right to vote with the 19th Amendment in 1920. Although many attendees of the Seneca Falls meeting were also active in the abolitionist movement, the gains made by the women's rights movement were not realized by women of color, particularly African-American women, until the 1960's. This tension was epitomized by **Sojouner Truth**, a former slave who became an eloquent activist for the rights of blacks and black women.

"THAT MAN OVER THERE SAYS THAT WOMEN NEED TO BE HELPED INTO CARRIAGES, AND LIFTED OVER DITCHES, AND TO HAVE THE BEST PLACE EVERYWHERE. NOBODY EVER HELPS ME INTO CARRIAGES, OR OVER MUD-PUDDLES, OR GIVES ME ANY BEST PLACE! AND AIN'T I A WOMAN? LOOK AT ME! LOOK AT MY ARM! I HAVE PLOUGHED AND PLANTED, AND GATHERED INTO BARNS, AND NO MAN COULD HEAD ME! AND AIN'T I A WOMAN?"
SOJOUNER TRUTH
"I COULD WORK AS MUCH AND EAT AS MUCH AS A MAN – WHEN I COULD GET IT – AND BEAR THE LASH AS WELL! AND AIN'T I A WOMAN? I HAVE BORNE 13 CHILDREN, AND SEEN MOST ALL SOLD OFF TO SLAVERY, AND WHEN I CRIED OUT WITH MY MOTHER'S GRIEF, NONE BUT JESUS HEARD ME! AND AIN'T I A WOMAN?"

WOMEN'S RIGHTS: THE FEMINIST MOVEMENTS

The voting rights movement is often considered the "first wave" of feminist movements, with the second wave coming in the 1960's and 70's, when women fought for equality in the workplace, their households, and their sexual lives. "Personal is political," was their rallying cry, connecting women's personal experiences to broader political structures and institutions. This period was a watershed time for legal protections and rights for women. Still, not every fight was won. The **Equal Rights Amendment (ERA)**, first proposed in the 1920's, which stated: "Equality of rights under the law shall not be denied or abridged by the United States or by any State on account of sex," was passed by Congress in 1972 but was not ratified by enough states, and, to this day, has yet to pass.

THE EQUAL CREDIT OPPORTUNITY ACT (1974) PROHIBITED BANKS FROM DENYING WOMEN THE RIGHT TO A CREDIT CARD ON THE BASIS ON THEIR SEX.
5412 7501 2345 0382
12/20
MS. ANNE SMITH
BETTY FRIEDAN
THE NATIONAL ORGANIZATION FOR WOMEN (NOW) WAS FOUNDED IN 1966, WITH THE GOAL OF "TAKING ACTION" TO BRING ABOUT EQUALITY FOR WOMEN.
Taking Action!
THE EQUAL PAY ACT (1963) ABOLISHED WAGE DISPARITY BASED ON SEX (ALTHOUGH WOMEN TODAY STILL EARN ONLY 83% OF WHAT MEN EARN).
$
$
RIGHT TO CHOOSE
THE SUPREME COURT DECISION IN ROE V. WADE (1973) PROTECTED A WOMAN'S RIGHT TO AN ABORTION.
THE PREGNANCY DISCRIMINATION ACT (1978) MEANT THAT EMPLOYERS COULD NO LONGER FIRE A WOMAN FOR BEING PREGNANT.

WOMEN'S RIGHTS: 3RD AND 4TH WAVES

In the 1960's, a black feminist movement argued that gender could not be understood outside the context of race and class, an idea later termed **intersectionality** by the legal scholar Kimberlé Crenshaw. This concept became a driving force in the "third wave" of feminism in the 1990's, which challenged the idea of a "universal woman," and focused on the diversity of personal identity. This movement found expression in a number of ways – one being the punk rock movement Riot grrrl, which directly confronted issues of (among other things) racism, homophobia, sexism, and sexual violence against women and girls, not only through music but also through direct grassroots mobilization.

There is now a "fourth wave" of feminism, which originated in around 2012 and which is primarily communicated by social media. It includes the **Me Too** movement, in which women shared experiences of sexual harassment and assault.

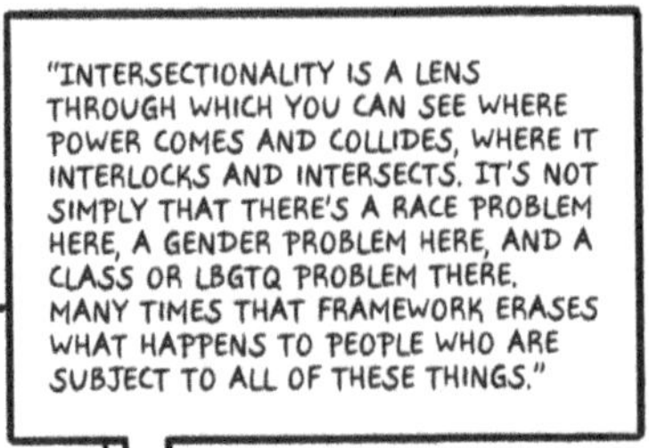

"INTERSECTIONALITY IS A LENS THROUGH WHICH YOU CAN SEE WHERE POWER COMES AND COLLIDES, WHERE IT INTERLOCKS AND INTERSECTS. IT'S NOT SIMPLY THAT THERE'S A RACE PROBLEM HERE, A GENDER PROBLEM HERE, AND A CLASS OR LBGTQ PROBLEM THERE. MANY TIMES THAT FRAMEWORK ERASES WHAT HAPPENS TO PEOPLE WHO ARE SUBJECT TO ALL OF THESE THINGS."

KIMBERLÉ CRENSHAW
@Alyssa_Milano
Follo
If you've been sexually harassed or assaulted write 'me too' as a reply to this tweet.
Me too.
Suggested by a friend: "If all the women who have been sexually harassed or assaulted wrote 'Me too.' as a status, we might give people a sense of the magnitude of the problem."
9:21 PM - 15 Oct 2017
24,436 RTs 52,972 LIKES
FOUNDED BY TARANA BURKE IN 2006, THE ME TOO MOVEMENT WENT VIRAL IN 2017.

LABOR MOVEMENT

Before the labor movement took hold in the late 1800's, there were few restrictions on work conditions in the United States. Workers could be required to work up to 18 hours a day in conditions without health or safety regulations, and the use of child labor was common. Strikes spread across the US in the 1870's to protest conditions, and the first wide-scale labor organizations formed – most notably the **American Federation of Labor (AFL)**, which formed in 1886 as a splinter organization from the earlier Knights of Labor. The AFL focused on the protection of skilled workers in the craft industry (an approach known as craft unionism). In 1935, workers who had been excluded from the AFL by its focus on craft unionism created the **Congress of Industrial Organizations (CIO)** . Its ethos was industrial unionism (where all workers in an industry are represented, regardless of skill). In 1955, the two organizations merged to form the AFL-CIO, which today is the largest labor organization in the US.

LGBT RIGHTS: MARRIAGE EQUALITY

On June 28, 1969, police in New York City raided a gay bar known as the Stonewall Inn to arrest individuals who were not wearing clothing that was deemed to correspond to their sex at birth. It resulted in a riot that lasted 6 days and sparked the modern gay rights movement. The struggle for equal rights for lesbian, gay, bisexual, and transgender (LGBT) people has made remarkable strides in the 50 years since the **Stonewall Riots**. One aspect of the movement is the push for marriage equality. Until 2015, states could deny same-sex partners the right to be married and thus deny them the accompanying benefits, such as the ability to make important medical decisions for a partner, to receive social security benefits upon a partner's death, to file joint tax returns, and to be included on a partner's health plan.

In 1970, Richard Baker and James Michael McConnell's application for a marriage license in Minneapolis was denied by a court clerk, on the basis that they were a same-sex couple. The couple sued in district court but their case was dismissed, as it also was when they appealed to the Minnesota Supreme Court and, then, the US Supreme Court (***Baker v. Nelson***, 1971). Whether or not to allow or recognize same-sex unions was left to the states, which varied in their stances towards the issue. In 1990, 3 same-sex couples sued in Hawaii for their right to marry. The state Supreme Court decided in 1993 that the case had merit, but it took 9 years for the case, ***Baehr v. Miike*** (1999), to be decided in favor of the plaintiffs and for the state's prohibition to be found unconstitutional. The initial 1993 ruling worried opponents, who pushed for the passage of the federal **Defense of Marriage Act (DOMA**, 1996), which defined marriage as being between a man and a woman and gave states the ability to ***not*** recognize marriages that were performed in other states.

The rush to push DOMA through before same-sex marriage was legalized in Hawaii was partly because of Article IV, Section I of the Constitution, which requires states to recognize and honor the "public Acts, Records, and judicial proceedings" (including marriage licenses) of other states. Section 2 of DOMA explicitly allowed states to bypass this, and Section 3 exempted the federal government. Edith Windsor challenged Section 3 in the courts when, in 2009, her wife passed away and the federal government refused her claim to the estate tax exemption for surviving spouses – leaving her with a federal tax bill of $363,000. In ***United States v. Windsor*** (2013) the court found in Windsor's favor, on the basis that Section 3 denied citizens due process. Two years later, in ***Obergefell v. Hodges*** the Supreme Court invalidated DOMA entirely, and recognized marriage as a fundamental right that could not be abridged by the states or federal government.

TRANS RIGHTS

While the movement for marriage equality has made great strides, many other rights for LGBTQ individuals have yet to be realized, such as the fight for the civil rights of transgender people. A person is **transgender**, or "trans," if they identify with a gender that differs from the sex they were assigned at birth (someone who identifies with their birth sex is considered **cisgender**). Unlike race, color, and religion, gender identity is not a nationally protected class, making it difficult for trans people to use the courts to advance their rights. Some states have legislated against discrimination on the basis of gender identity; however, trans people face many daily battles, from the ability to use a bathroom that corresponds with their gender identity, to discrimination in custody decisions, or some states' requirement of gender reassignment surgery in order to change the gender on their official ID.

CIVIL RIGHTS

The civil rights movement of the 1950's and 60's was, like the feminist movement, a struggle for equality not just at the level of federal laws but also in the workplace, the neighborhood, and the home. Black people in the US experienced overt violence and explicit bias – from redlining, in which banks and realtors denied blacks the ability to buy a home, to racial profiling and harassment by the police, mass incarceration, inferior schools, and lower pay and opportunities for advancement. They also faced systemic racism and **implicit bias** – unconscious attitudes and stereotypes held by individuals based on the characteristics of another person, such as race. The civil rights movement sought change not only in formal institutions (through policy change) but also in informal institutions – society's norms, beliefs, and understandings about race.

The birth of the civil rights movement is often attributed to **Rosa Parks**, who in 1955 refused to give up her seat on a bus to a white passenger in Montgomery, Alabama and sparked the 381-day Montgomery Bus Boycott – leading the Supreme Court to declare in 1956 that segregated buses were unconstitutional. One wing of the movement was led by the **Reverend Martin Luther King Jr.**, who advocated for change through nonviolent protest and helped found the Southern Christian Leadership Conference (SCLC) to organize the movement across the South. Not all civil rights activists agreed with King's non-violent tactics and integrationist goals. The influential leader **Malcolm X** was a proponent of **Black Nationalism** – the belief that blacks constituted a nation which should seek independence and resist assimilation to white culture.

While black activism in the US didn't start with the civil rights movement (for example, scholars have identified over 250 slave revolts and conspiracies during the era of slavery), it was a remarkable time in terms of bringing about rapid policy changes. During this time, a key Supreme Court decision was challenged – that of *Plessy v. Ferguson* (1896), which had stated that the segregation of whites and blacks was constitutional as long as what was being provided to different races was "separate but equal." That decision had been used to justify a host of discriminatory, segregationist practices, and equal resources weren't provided to blacks because the segregation made those resources de facto unequal.

When John F. Kennedy was elected president in 1960, the African-American electorate was hopeful that he would champion legislation for their equality. Sympathetic as he was to their plight, Kennedy did not immediately move to pass new laws, sensing that he did not have sufficient support from members of Congress. However, as civil rights activists faced increasing brutality for their protests, he became more compelled towards action. For example, when activists known as "**Freedom Riders**" took buses down South to protest continued segregation in interstate travel facilities and were attacked by mobs, he sent federal troops to protect them, and when the City Commissioner in Birmingham, Alabama used fire hoses and police dogs against peaceful protesters, Kennedy began drafting comprehensive civil rights legislation. Unfortunately, he was assassinated before it could be passed. It was under Lyndon B. Johnson, his successor, that the **Civil Rights Act** (1964) finally passed. The Act comprised 11 sections or "Titles." Title I stipulated that any requirements to vote be applied evenly among all races (with the **Voting Rights Act** of 1965, barriers to voting, such as literacy tests, were eliminated entirely). Other parts of the legislation include:

BLACK LIVES MATTER

Just as the fight for civil rights didn't begin in the 1950's and 60's, it also didn't end there. The Black Lives Matter (**BLM**) movement began after the 2013 acquittal of George Zimmerman, who was accused of murdering an unarmed black teenager named Trayvon Martin. The movement gained force in 2014 after the shooting of another unarmed black teenager, Michael Brown, by a white police officer in Ferguson, Missouri didn't result in an indictment against the police officer. The movement addressed systemic racism, police brutality, and other concerns of African Americans, such as racial inequality in the criminal justice system. BLM now has at least 40 international, decentralized chapters. Local groups don't have to get "official" sanctioning for their tactics, but they do have to undergo training before using "BLM" in their group's name. In this way, the BLM movement can be said to encompass an expansive agenda, based on principles of racial justice.

OPPOSITION TO AND EVOLUTION OF BLACK LIVES MATTER

The tactics and messages of the BLM movement are controversial. Opponents began to use the phrase "All Lives Matter," arguing that BLM's exclusive focus on black lives ignored the fact that people of all colors could be victims of violence. Similarly, a "Blue Lives Matter" trend began after 2 police officers in New York City were killed in 2014. Proponents were in part reacting to what they felt was an anti-police sentiment in the BLM movement. Recently, BLM has broadened its tactics, from protests and disruption to working to communicate empathy for black issues in the media.

In general, race and party affiliation tend to predict favorable or unfavorable feelings towards the BLM movement. According to a 2017 Harvard-Harris survey, 21% of Republicans and 35% of white voters have a favorable view, compared to 65% of Democrats and 83% of black voters.

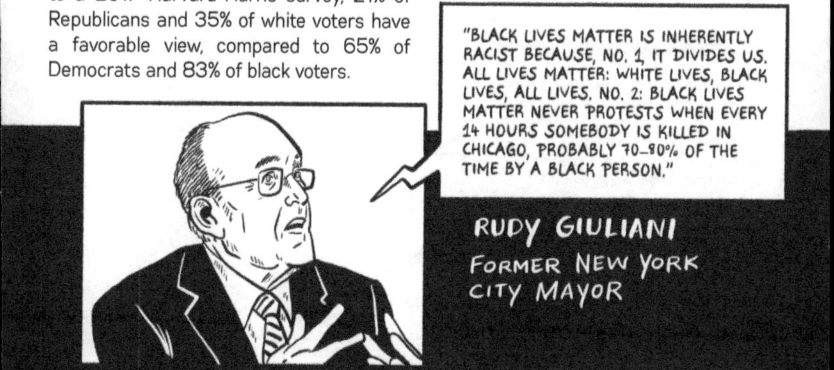

"BLACK LIVES MATTER IS INHERENTLY RACIST BECAUSE, NO. 1, IT DIVIDES US. ALL LIVES MATTER: WHITE LIVES, BLACK LIVES, ALL LIVES. NO. 2: BLACK LIVES MATTER NEVER PROTESTS WHEN EVERY 14 HOURS SOMEBODY IS KILLED IN CHICAGO, PROBABLY 70–80% OF THE TIME BY A BLACK PERSON."
RUDY GIULIANI
FORMER NEW YORK CITY MAYOR
"PEOPLE ARE CHANNELING THEIR ENERGY INTO ORGANIZING LOCALLY, RECOGNIZING THAT IN TRUMP'S AMERICA, OUR COMMUNITIES ARE UNDER DIRECT ATTACK."
ALICIA GARZA
CO-FOUNDER OF BLM

THE TEA PARTY

The Tea Party is not an actual party but a conservative grassroots movement centered around core principles of lowering taxes, balancing the federal budget, and removing restrictions to personal freedom. There is some debate over the origins of the movement, but one commonly cited origin is with a speech by the financial analyst Rick Santelli during a 2009 TV interview, in which he railed against proposed government assistance for individuals with houses in foreclosure, suggesting that in response he was going to organize a tea party in Chicago where they would be dumping "derivative securities." The allusion to the Revolutionary War's symbolic tea party gained traction, and local Tea Party groups began to form. While the core principles focus on a few key agenda items, their social media messages encompass a wide range of conservative issues such as support of anti-immigration policy, pro-Christian messages, and allegations of Democratic voter fraud.

"WASHINGTON IS HORRIBLY BROKEN. WE ARE ENCOUNTERING A DAY OF RECKONING, AND THIS MOVEMENT, THIS TEA PARTY MOVEMENT, IS A MESSAGE TO WASHINGTON THAT WE'RE UNHAPPY AND THAT WE WANT THINGS DONE DIFFERENTLY."
Rand Paul
"I BELIEVE IN THIS MOVEMENT. AMERICA IS READY FOR ANOTHER REVOLUTION. IT IS SO INSPIRING TO SEE REAL PEOPLE, NOT INSIDE-THE-BELTWAY PROFESSIONALS, STAND UP AND SPEAK OUT FOR COMMONSENSE, CONSERVATIVE PRINCIPLES."
Sarah Palin

THE TEA PARTY: LEGACY

The Tea Party movement reached its height in 2010 and '11, with 30% of Americans in a Gallup poll saying they supported it. Its popularity was based partly on its ability to activate and harness the energy of people in the US who felt threatened or concerned by the liberal policies of the Obama administration. The Tea Party's work centered around 2 key principles: 1) utilizing small local groups (often as few as 10 members) who were highly dedicated and vocal; and 2) maintaining a "defensive" strategy hyper-focused on blocking Obama's legislation, demanding that their elected officials push that opposition, and punishing legislators who did not deliver. While many of the original supporters in Congress are now allied with other movements, the Tea Party's populist message continues in other conservative groups, and its grassroots mobilization strategy continues to be emulated (such as by the liberal movement, **Indivisible**).

THE ALT-RIGHT "MOVEMENT"?

As previously mentioned, Steve Bannon's stint as the White House Chief Strategist brought attention to what is known as the "alt-right" movement, of which Bannon was seen by many to be an enabler, if not an active part (a perception not helped by Bannon making an offhand comment in 2016 that his ***Breitbart News*** was a "platform for the alt-right"). The term "alt-right" was popularized by the white nationalist Richard Spencer, but it's vague, encompassing a wide range of individuals with extremist ideologies, who frequently express themselves in online forums. According to the Southern Poverty Law Center, a nonprofit dedicated to tracking hate groups, "Alt-righters eschew 'establishment' conservatism, skew young, and embrace white ethnonationalism." Because of the variety of ideologies encompassed by the term, as well as a lack of formal organization, one could question whether the alt-right can be called a movement, ***per se***.

THE KKK

In contrast to the alt-right, certain hate groups do have a clearly stated, shared ideology and, unfortunately, a long history of galvanizing action. The Ku Klux Klan (KKK), formed in 1866, is one of the oldest white supremacist hate groups and has gone through cycles of revival and decline since its founding. It is no longer a single group headed by one leader but comprises at least four primary splinter groups and many more small, local groups – with an estimated 22 states having at least one active chapter. **The Anti-Defamation League (ADL)** estimates that the KKK has around 3,000 members in the nation, and that at least half of its groups formed after 2014. This, the ADL points out, is not necessarily a sign of a surge in membership but that many groups form and dissolve rather quickly.

NEO-NAZI GROUPS

Although it is the oldest group, the Klan's members comprise a small minority of white supremacist groups nationwide. According to the Southern Poverty Law Center, in 2018 the number of white supremacist groups rose to 600, of which 120 were neo-Nazi groups – a 22% rise from just a year earlier. Post-war neo-Nazism in the US originated in 1959, when George Lincoln Rockwell founded the American Nazi Party. Neo-Nazi groups share the ideas of the German Nazi party, including xenophobia, anti-Semitism, homophobia, ultranationalism, and a fascist political ideology. In the United States the ability of neo-Nazis to express their views is protected by the 1st Amendment provision for freedom of speech, and they often take advantage of this fact to provide a platform for neo-Nazis in Europe, where such groups are illegal.

ANTIFA

A movement has grown known as **Antifa** (short for "antifascist"), which stands in opposition to fascist and other hate groups. It gained a lot of recent attention (and controversy) for the tactics it took in opposition to the election of Donald Trump, but Antifa's roots go back to the 1920's and 30's, in response to the rise of pro-fascist groups in the US. The movement declined after the end of WWII but experienced a revival in the 70's and 80's in the punk scene in the US and Britain. It is not a centralized movement but a loose network, with an emphasis on direct action (both violent and nonviolent), such as going to where neo-Nazi and other hate groups are holding events and using force to disrupt their activities. Because of the group's association with violence, the Department of Homeland Security under the Trump administration reportedly labeled them a "domestic terrorist" group in 2017.

TOWARDS A MORE PERFECT UNION

While the open existence of hate groups in the United States is abhorrent, they comprise just one small fraction of the people who become motivated to join groups in order to shape the future of their communities and the nation. Sometimes these groups form after a defining moment, as was the case with the gay rights movement after Stonewall. Other times, it is more difficult to pinpoint an exact moment of activation, as the strength of the movement is the fruition of years of grassroots organization. Regardless of how they come about, the fact is that these movements have moved the United States progressively towards realizing its founding principle, as stated in the Declaration of Independence, that everyone has the right to life, liberty, and the pursuit of happiness.

CONCLUSION

As we have seen throughout this book, the great social movements that have shaped American history are just one way that state and society interact to produce change in institutions. The formal rules of the game, as expressed by the laws that govern human interaction, may seem static at times, but when we examine them at all levels – from the family and the neighborhood to the constant interchange of ideas between citizens and their local and state politicians and bureaucrats – we see that they are in constant evolution. It happens in moments and daily struggles which are often overlooked by textbooks, but that are no less real to those who experience them.

THERE'S STILL A LOT OF WORK TO BE DONE IN HOW WE TELL THE STORY OF BLACK POLITICS.
AND NATIVE AMERICAN POLITICS. THERE'S MORE TO OUR HISTORY THAN THE TRAIL OF TEARS.

In this book we have tried to provide both a bird's eye and a ground-level view of how this evolutionary process works, emphasizing how it feels to the ordinary American.

I STILL HAVE SO MANY QUESTIONS.
THAT'S NEVER GOING TO CHANGE! JUST KEEP ASKING THEM AND TRYING TO LEARN MORE.
HONESTLY, I DON'T KNOW IF I LIKE THE GOVERNMENT MORE OR LESS AFTER LEARNING ALL OF THIS!
I GET THAT. WE NEED TO BE VIGILANT, BUT WE NEED TO KNOW MORE ABOUT HOW WE GOT TO THIS POINT.

THERE WERE TIMES YOU GUYS REALLY ANNOYED ME BUT ALSO TIMES YOU SURPRISED ME. I APPRECIATE YOUR BEING OPEN TO HAVING A DIALOGUE.
WELL, THANKS. ALTHOUGH I DISAGREE WITH YOU, I ADMIRE YOUR PASSION FOR THE THINGS YOU BELIEVE IN.
I DON'T GET A CHANCE TO HEAR PERSPECTIVES LIKE YOURS VERY OFTEN. I HAVE A LOT TO THINK ABOUT.
"FOR THIS IS WHAT AMERICA IS ALL ABOUT. IT IS THE UNCROSSED DESERT AND THE UNCLIMBED RIDGE. IT IS THE STAR THAT IS NOT REACHED AND THE HARVEST THAT IS SLEEPING IN THE UNPLOWED GROUND."
PRESIDENT Lyndon Baines Johnson